PASSIVE INVESTING MADE SIMPLE

JAKE GINO

— *Present* —

Dear Reader,

This book is presented solely for educational purposes. The author and publisher are not offering it as legal, accounting, or other professional services advice. While best efforts have been used in preparing this book, the author and publisher make no representations or warranties of any kind and assume no liabilities of any kind with respect to the accuracy or completeness of the contents and specifically disclaim any implied warranties of merchantability or fitness of use for a particular purpose.

Neither the author nor the publisher shall be held liable or responsible to any person or entity with respect to any loss or incidental or consequential damages caused, or alleged to have been caused, directly or indirectly, by the information or programs contained herein. No warranty may be created or extended by sales representatives or written sales materials.

Every business scenario is different, and the advice and strategies contained herein may not be suitable for your situation. You should seek the services of a competent legal professional before making use of any of the techniques in this book.

TABLE OF CONTENTS

PASSIVE INVESTING MADE SIMPLE

HOW TO CREATE WEALTH AND PASSIVE INCOME THROUGH APARTMENT SYNDICATIONS

ANTHONY VICINO & DAN KRUEGER

FOREWORD

I had the privilege of being introduced to Anthony by his partner Dan a couple of years ago. Dan, a successful investor and entrepreneur looking to scale his real estate portfolio, joined the Jake and Gino community in 2019. Dan was the ideal fit for the community, a motivated, inspirational, intelligent, and articulate person ready to take that next big step.

When Anthony joined the community, I knew instantly that we were kindred spirits. His last name Vicino means "close" in Italian, and that is the connection I felt with him and with Dan. The partners possessed an affinity for personal development, and they both studied the same thought leaders and read the same books that were a huge influence on my own life. Whenever I talk with these guys, I always emerge smarter and more motivated.

Anthony and Dan possessed another trait that instantly attracted me. Even though they were high-level performers and had achieved success, they were coachable and open to learning new concepts. The partners exhibited the growth mindset, a belief in their ability to increase their abilities through hard work and determination.

I credit most of my success in life to surrounding myself with amazing people just like Anthony and Dan.

When Anthony approached me to collaborate on this project, it was a no-brainer. He is a gifted writer with an amazing track record both real estate and entrepreneurship. I knew that the real estate world would benefit tremendously from this book, and it has been a privilege to participate in this project.

What I truly enjoy most about this book is its approach to breaking down apartment investing simply and clearly. They lay out the step-by-step framework on how to passively invest in real estate, all while simplifying the often-confusing strategy of syndication.

If you have found it difficult to begin investing in apartments, look no further. Anthony and Dan have truly made passive investing simple for me and for you.

MIH!

Gino Barbaro

PART ONE

THE PATH TO FINANCIAL FREEDOM

CHAPTER 1

IT'S REALLY NOT THAT COMPLICATED

"90% of all millionaires become so through owning real estate."

— Andrew Carnegie

Have you ever driven through a major city, looked up at all of the buildings, and wondered, *Who owns all these?*

For the first thirty years of my life, I (Anthony) sure didn't. Then one day, driving into downtown Minneapolis, something changed. A eureka moment that created a paradigm shift in how I viewed the world (or, more specifically, the real estate) around me.

On that day of all days, for whatever reason, a question popped into my head: *Who the heck owns all these buildings?*

The answer, which I would later discover, took me completely by surprise. Yes, big corporations, REITs (Real Estate Investment Trusts), and uber-wealthy individuals own their fair share. But it shocked me to discover that investors no different than you and me owned as much (if not more) of that real estate.

Busy working professionals with careers and families and softball leagues... And you want to know the craziest part of all?

Most of these people have never dealt with a single tenant, they've never dealt with a broken toilet in the middle of the night, and they've never had to make a single mortgage payment themselves. Most of these investors are completely passive.

But although they're passive, these investors still benefit from all the things that make real estate such a powerful investment vehicle. The appreciation, the cash flow, the tax benefits, the stability, the hedge against inflation, the...

You know, this is starting to sound like one of those too good to be true, *"But wait, there's more!"* sales pitches. Let's back up.

If you're new to real estate investing (and you're anything like us) then you're probably feeling eager, excited, and a little overwhelmed.

I began my real estate journey by spending months sifting through the mountain of information available on all the different ways you can make (and lose) money through real estate investing. I attended seminars, conferences, and meet-up groups, spoke with countless other investors, and consumed a constant stream of podcasts. Oh, and I read practically every book on the topic.

Every piece of content I consumed birthed three new questions. The more I learned, the more I realized just how little I knew.

With all the horror stories about some guy's uncle losing his shirt in a real estate scheme, I needed to be certain I knew what I was doing before jumping in. Maybe that's what brought you here.

Through time, experience, and a handful of awesome mentors, we've learned some things that'll fast-track your education, help narrow your field of focus, and give you the confidence to move forward into real estate and start building generational wealth for you and your family.

Are you ready for lesson number one? Here it is: *real estate investing isn't terribly complicated.*

I know it doesn't feel that way when you're first starting out, but that's only because you're still drinking from the fire hose of possibility.

The first step to simplifying your real estate journey is to narrow your focus. To that end, in this book, you'll learn everything you need to know about passively investing in value-add apartment syndications.

Once complete, you'll have the tools and knowledge necessary to vet exceptional operators, identify an amazing deal, build a rock-star team, and passively fund incredible investment opportunities.

To us, value-add apartment syndications are the simplest, most reliable, and most profitable way to invest. We've helped dozens of investors on the path to financial freedom through this powerful investment vehicle, and we're excited to show how *you* can, too.

Ready to get started?

Wait, wait, wait... Okay, first, let's lay some groundwork and establish the question probably burning in your mind: **Who the heck are these guys and why should I bother listening to them?**

Great question.

Our stories are probably not terribly different from your own. We were both raised on the prescription that the *correct path* through life means going to school, getting a degree, working hard, investing in your 401(k) for retirement, and then riding off into the sunset at sixty-five to sip margaritas on an exotic beach.

Neither of us, as it turns out, wanted to wait that long to start living life on our terms. So we went in search of a better way.

DAN'S STORY

Dan grew up on the movie *Wall Street* and became obsessed with the idea of high-energy trading floors filled with fast action, huge returns, and seemingly limitless possibilities. Logically, therefore, he followed that path to college and studied finance and economics. He was a studious young lad who followed the "correct path" to a corporate finance career, making a comfortable $50,000/year salary straight out of college.

...Which eventually led to a rude awakening. Turns out this "high salary" barely got him to first base. Each month, after paying student loans, his car loan, rent, and other bills, he had practically nothing left over.

So Dan started a side hustle coaching fitness and nutrition to help people take control over their physical health and start living more fulfilling lives. In short order, that side hustle started generating a solid income that was directly correlated to his efforts. That is, his inputs clearly impacted his outputs.

The entrepreneurial bug had bitten.

Dan dove into learning and consumed everything he could get his hands on about business development, sales, and personal development. He obsessively listened to podcasts and audiobooks while continuing to plug away at his corporate job.

A few short years later and that side hustle generated more income than the W-2. From that moment forward, he began mentally checking out of the corporate world.

That is, until 2017, when he stumbled upon a free copy of the purple book. Dan had heard people talk about *Rich Dad, Poor Dad* before, but it seemed so cheesy. This time, however, he decided, "What the heck, it's free," and gave it a shot.

This led to a fundamental shift in how he thought about the world, personal finance, and wealth.

Think about that. A guy educated in finance and economics, who'd spent his entire working career in corporate finance, couldn't see the better way sitting right in front of him the whole time.

That better way was real estate.

Now it was time to consume everything on *that* topic. It quickly became evident that there are countless ways to make money in real estate, and they're all potentially viable, but if you want to succeed, you have to choose one and focus. Upon learning about all the different types of real estate investing, one stood above and beyond all the rest for Dan: *multifamily apartment buildings.*

Dan knew from his nutrition coaching business that knowledge is only potential power. To have any effect, it must be applied.

So Dan applied his education and went shopping. By the end of 2017, he had purchased his first deal, a six-unit apartment building, for $475,000. Within nine months he'd renovated the property, forced massive appreciation, and then executed a cash-out refinance that returned the majority of his initial investment.

With fresh capital back in hand, he purchased his second property. And that's what we call maximizing the velocity of your capital.

The stars were aligned. Dan and his wife didn't have any children at the time and were earning enough supplemental income between his side hustle and his wife's full-time job to keep the lights on while Dan left his corporate finance career and plunged headlong into real estate investing.

Millions of dollars' worth of acquisitions later, and he's never looked back.

ANTHONY'S STORY

When I was a child, my dad made it clear to me that I was going to college. It was a foregone conclusion. So when the time came, I grabbed a degree in psychology. Then one in English. Then another in religion. It wasn't clear what I wanted to do or where I wanted to go; I just stayed on the path ascribed to me and kept trudging forward.

One thing was always clear to me, however: I'm a bad employee.

See, I have severe ADHD (Attention Deficit Hyperactivity Disorder), and for the first twenty-five years of my life I struggled desperately to control my scattershot mind. I was unfocused, unreliable, and inconsistent. This all but guaranteed I would never cut it in the corporate world or working for somebody else. The only solution would be to forge my own path forward.

So I obsessively studied psychology, peak performance, and habit formation for years. And slowly but surely, I started gaining the upper hand on my biology. Understanding how my quirky brain works—and, most importantly, how to use it to my advantage—was the great turning point in my life.

From there, I went on to travel the world as a professional rock climber, spending the better part of a decade visiting the most incredible places the planet has to offer. Along the way, I picked up the pen and started writing. A few years later, I published my first science fiction and fantasy novel. Then another. And another.

And then one day a friend asked me if I'd like to build a business with him and I discovered something that changed the trajectory of my life. It turns out that all the systems I'd created to help me take control of my ADHD and become a functioning member of society were also perfectly suited for building businesses, something I never would've imagined when I was a kid.

A few short years later, and we'd built three multi-million-dollar companies from the ground up.

It was around the time that I was building a manufacturing company that specializes in polyurethane cast molding that I was hit by a question. I remember driving into downtown Minneapolis, staring up at the brilliantly backlit skyline and wondering for the very first time in my life: **Who owns all these skyscrapers?**

At the time, I knew practically nothing about real estate. I had passively invested in a couple small residential properties and during college I had helped my roommate and his dad flip a couple single-family homes, but my knowledge of commercial real estate was effectively zero.

Now, make no mistake, I have no interest in actually buying a skyscraper. But in trying to answer that question, I discovered something pretty fascinating: multifamily real estate.

Shortly thereafter I bought a triplex, and within a year I'd made $125,000 on that single property—but you'll hear all about that later.

OUR STORY

Dan and I met at a local networking event, though at the time neither of us was specifically looking for a partner. It wasn't until many months later that we realized the powerful synergy existing at the intersection of our personalities and skill sets.

We have complementary skills coupled with compatible personalities. Dan is the analytical and detail-oriented one, whereas I tend toward creativity and the big picture. Where Dan's a wizard with numbers, I'm pretty good at building systems designed to scale.

Together we formed Invictus Capital, a vertically integrated multifamily acquisition firm based in the Twin Cities, and have never looked back.

But it's not just about the real estate for us.

We were fortunate to wake up from the American dream, but most people don't realize the dream is just that: a *dream*. Most people never wake up. Saddest of all? Most people don't realize there's a better dream, one that could easily be turned into reality if only they just knew and put into action a few pieces of key knowledge. A dream enabling you to take control over your financial destiny by creating multiple passive income streams. A dream enabling you to achieve financial freedom decades earlier than most.

The best part? It's all so simple.

Our goal is to help wake people from the American dream.

That you're holding this book now suggests you're ready to wake up.

So what do you say we stop hitting the snooze button and learn a better way?

CHAPTER 2

FINANCIAL FREEDOM IS EASIER THAN YOU THINK

"Real wealth is not about money. Real wealth is: not having to go to meetings, not having to spend time with jerks, not being locked into status games, not feeling like you have to say 'yes,' not worrying about others claiming your time and energy. Real wealth is about freedom."

— James Clear

Sparta is a black ball of meowing fluff. He has cartoonishly large eyes and wants nothing more in this world than to be held. When I open my office door, he's there, ready for his opportunity to jump on my shoulder. If I'm sitting anywhere in the house, he's in my lap. Always.

This cat is needy, but that's okay because he's adorable.

A couple years ago, Sparta got sick. Really sick. He ate something stupid that his body couldn't process, and it was killing him. He's not the smartest cat, but we don't hold that against him, 'cause, again, he is quite cute.

On Christmas Day, we learned that my best furry little buddy would die unless we performed a fairly routine surgery. The price tag on that fairly routine surgery, however, was anything but fairly routine for us at that time.

We were now required to do some intense mental calculus to determine the dollar value of Sparta's life. How do you quantify the value of a loved one?

Sure, he was just a cat, but he was *my* cat. My faithful companion who never left my side, trusting me to take care of him. Isn't that the job we signed up for when we brought him into our home?

In the end, after much mental anguish, we couldn't justify the expense. And so we took Sparta home, made him comfortable, gave him an endless supply of cuddles, and said our goodbyes. I mentally prepared myself for the next day, when we would take him in for one last visit to the vet and then that would be it. No more furry little buddy.

The next morning we awoke, prepared to take Sparta into the vet, but something had changed in the night.

Sparta was somehow better. Completely better.

Huzzah, the power of love saves the day, right?

Well, whatever the reason for Sparta's remarkable recovery, this section isn't about pontificating on life's innumerable existential mysteries. It's about determining your *why*.

Most people pursue real estate investing for its unrivaled ability to generate wealth. No other investment vehicle has created more millionaires over the course of human history than real estate, and there's a reason for that.

"Financial freedom" is a popular phrase that means something slightly different to everybody. At their core, most people don't actually care about being "wealthy." They simply want the ability to live life on their terms, without the specter of work, bills, and every other expense of life looming over them.

For Dan, financial freedom meant that the net monthly income from his passive investments exceeded his monthly expenses. Once this was achieved, the perpetual money machine had been ignited, requiring no more input (i.e., work) from the operator (i.e., Dan). This meant Dan has more time for his family and for the things in life he's truly passionate about.

For me, financial freedom means never having to do mental jujitsu to determine the dollar value of a loved one's life (even if that loved one is just a cat). Financial freedom means money is never the reason I can't help someone I love.

Your reasons for pursuing financial freedom are probably different than either Dan's or mine. Whatever your reason, it's critical you know your *why* and use its guiding light to illuminate your path forward.

Don't settle into an investment vehicle that's not headed to your desired destination. You wouldn't take a job without considering your career, fulfillment, or long-term goals, right?

Maybe you want to make enough to pay your monthly bills and quit the W-2 so you can use your time traveling the world with family. Maybe you have an aging parent you want to support when the time comes. Regardless of the goal, passive investing in apartments can help get you there.

Throughout this book, you'll learn all the reasons why multifamily is such an incredible wealth-generating vehicle. But before we get to that, take some time to consider *what* financial freedom means to you and *why* it's so important. Get crystal clear on exactly why you want this. Next, write it down on a piece of paper and place that note someplace where you can't help but see it every single day.

The most surefire way of turning your dreams into reality is by keeping those dreams pinned to the forefront of your mind and then pursuing them with relentless focus.

Now that you have your why, let's look at a fun case study showing one way you could achieve your goals by investing in value-add apartment syndications. In this example, we're going to invest $50,000 in one apartment syndication every year for the next five years in a row.

Each year we'll earn cash-on-cash returns of 7%, 10%, 15%, 15%, 15% and plan for cash-out refinances in year three that return 35% of our initial capital. Oh yeah, and we'll sell the property in year five. All told, the average projected **internal rate of return (IRR) is 20%.**

Wait, what?

Okay, we threw out a bunch of terms that may or may not make sense to you depending on where you are in your education. Don't worry, by the end of this book you're going to speak the lingo and understand everything about this deal. For now, don't get lost in the jargon, just watch how your investment grows.

Year	Number of active Deals	Cash Invested	Distributions Taken	Distributions Reinvested	Cash Flow	Refi Proceeds	Sales Proceeds	Equity	Cumulative Income
2020	1	$50,000.00	$–	$–	$3,500.00	$–	$–	$50,000.00	$3,500.00
2021	2	$46,500.00	$–	$3,500.00	$10,100.00	$–	$–	$105,000.00	$13,600.00
2022	3	$39,900.00	$–	$10,100.00	$16,550.00	$17,500.00	$–	$148,000.00	$47,650.00
2023	4	$15,950.00	$–	$34,050.00	$23,645.00	$17,500.00	$–	$195,300.00	$88,795.00
2024	5	$8,855.00	$–	$41,145.00	$31,449.50	$17,500.00	$52,030.00	$195,300.00	$189,774.00
2025	5	$–	$50,979.50	$50,000.00	$31,449.50	$17,500.00	$52,030.00	$195,300.00	$290,754.00

We'll need $50,000 to invest in year one, which of course is not an insignificant amount of money. If you're wondering where on Earth you'll come up with that type of cash, fear not—in a later chapter we'll share some places you might be surprised to discover you had the necessary funds hiding all along. In that chapter, we'll share how Dan and I both solved the capital issue to acquire our own first assets.

Now, to the numbers.

In year one we'll earn a cash-on-cash return of 7%, which produces $3,500 of cash flow for the year. Because we're diligent investors, we'll reinvest all that money and, in year two, we'll only need to produce another $46,500 to fund our next deal.

Roll forward one more year and we're earning returns on two properties for a grand total of $10,100 worth of cash flow. Again, we roll that money forward, and in year three we only need an additional $39,900 to fund the full $50,000 investment.

Are you starting to see how this works?

Good, because things really take off in year three, when we introduce the cash-out refinance, which returns a conservative 35% of our initial year one capital. If we add up the proceeds from our year three refinance ($17,500) and the cumulative cash flow ($16,550) across all properties, we're left having to raise only an additional $15,950 to fully fund our year four investment of $50,000.

Notice how the hurdle keeps getting lower and lower? That's the power of compounding effects.

Let's rinse and repeat with more cash flow and another refinance going into year five, and then it's time to hit the rocket boosters and sell that year one asset.

At the end of year five, we've made $31,449 from cash flow, $17,500 from a refinance, and $52,030 from selling our year one asset, for a cumulative income of $100,979. And with that, we've officially ignited the perpetual passive-cash-flow-generating machine.

From year five onward, our passive income generates enough to fund the following year's $50,000 investment while *also* earning enough to withdraw an additional $50,000 for living expenses, vacation, or, our personal favorite, reinvesting that money into our perpetual-passive-cash-flow-generating machine.

We hear you mumbling over there, *"This seems too good to be true."* You're right to be skeptical. Over the coming pages, we'll break down each aspect of the multifamily engine to equip you with the necessary tools, judgment, and insights necessary for you to arrive at your own conclusion.

The point of this exercise was to show that financial freedom isn't as far off (or unobtainable) as most people imagine. You don't need millions of dollars. A moderate amount of capital diligently applied consistently in solid investments will get you to the promised land surprisingly quickly.

Of course, not all investment vehicles are created equal. You need to do your homework and only fund the right deals with the right operators.

We subscribe to the Warren Buffet rules of investing: **"Rule number one is don't lose money. Rule number two is to never forget rule number one."**

And these rules couldn't be more true. Regardless of where you are in your investing journey, principal preservation is critical.

Throughout the rest of this book, we'll unpack how to determine whether a deal has the potential to deliver exceptional risk-adjusted returns, though it might surprise you to find that we spend more time talking about operators.

Why?

Because we believe you should bet on the jockey, not the horse.

Yes, the horse absolutely matters, but a great jockey isn't going to get on a mediocre horse. Furthermore, a great jockey knows how to get the most from their steed.

A terrible jockey, on the other hand, could mount the second coming of Secretariat and it wouldn't do any good. They're more likely to fall off and break their neck than they are to win.

All right, that's a whole lot of horse metaphor. Here's the point: We would rather partner with great operators on what appears to be a mediocre deal than pair with terrible operators on what appears to be a stellar deal. That's why we'll spend so much time in this book on the subject of finding and vetting operators.

But wait, we're getting ahead of ourselves. We've made some glaring assumptions—namely that you understand and agree with us that apartments are the best investment vehicle.

This isn't a fair assumption on our part. So next up, let's look at the apartment syndication landscape from a 50,000-foot view and answer the all-important question: **Why apartments?**

PART TWO

APARTMENT SYNDICATIONS

CHAPTER 3

WHY APARTMENTS?

"Real estate cannot be lost or stolen, nor can it be carried away. Purchased with common sense, paid for in full, and managed with reasonable care, it is about the safest investment in the world."

— Franklin D. Roosevelt

The first property I actively managed was a triplex that I house-hacked. That means I lived in one unit while renting out the other two to offset my living expenses and mortgage payment. Functionally, I lived for free, had my mortgage paid down, and benefited from all the tax breaks.

The triplex was a fantastic asset that generated an outstanding return. But despite this, the property had some significant issues.

For example, if a tenant moved out, my occupancy rate dropped by 33% and my monthly income took a massive hit. During these periods, the asset no longer sustained itself, which meant money had to come out of *my* pocket to keep things running.

Now, the returns were solid. Every month that both rental units were occupied, that property generated a couple hundred dollars' worth of cash flow. A great return, but not the sort of passive income that made a significant impact on the quality of my life. Not to mention that, if the boiler went out or a hole magically appeared in the roof, all that cash flow would simply vanish.

That's the inherent issue with small properties. The margins aren't big enough to justify implementing professional systems or hiring contractors, so you end up doing most things yourself (like dealing with bounty hunters in the middle of the night. Don't worry, we'll get to that in a bit).

By far the biggest issue I had with this little triplex, however, was the fact that I had absolutely no control over how much it was worth.

Case in point: I bought the property for $246,500 and refinanced it nine months later for $375,000 after putting less than $10,000 into it. That's $125,000 of value in the blink of an eye, and it came as a complete surprise.

How was that possible? Had the property really become so much more valuable in such a short period of time?

To put it bluntly, no, it didn't.

See, small properties (under five units) are valued based on *comparables.* The value of your building is influenced by what similar buildings within a particular radius have recently sold for. If you own a primary residence, you'll be familiar with this form of valuation.

It doesn't matter how well you operate your asset, it's worth about the same as the identical property across the street, regardless of how poorly your neighbor managed their asset.

These limitations were unacceptable to me. I didn't want a full-time job managing tenants, I didn't want to constantly worry about the next thing that might break, and I sure as heck wanted to have *some* control over the value of my building.

I returned to the drawing board to learn everything I could about the different asset classes and business models within real estate. I searched high and low for something that would offer five things in particular: cash flow, appreciation, control, stability, and tax benefits.

Which led me to—you guessed it—apartments!

STABILITY

Stability means a couple of different things to us.

First, assets prone to wild fluctuations in value (like the stock market) lack stability. We're pretty risk-averse. We seek steady, predictable valuations and returns. When it comes to investing, we hate surprises and volatility.

Remember how my top-line revenue would decrease by 33% whenever a tenant moved out of that triplex? With apartment buildings, the effects of one tenant moving out are far less impactful.

One tenant moving out of a hundred-unit building means we still collect 99% of our effective gross income (EGI). That means consistent, predictable returns.

Second, apartments are stable in that they fulfill a fundamental human need: shelter. Unlike stocks, or gold, or bitcoin, people *need* a place to live. There's always a demand for housing.

In recent years that demand has only increased, as both millennials and baby boomers increasingly move away from buying and owning their primary residences. Instead, across the board, Americans are downsizing their living, moving closer to urban centers, and placing a high premium on flexibility and freedom of movement.

Fewer and fewer people want to be tied down to a single-family home. As a result, we're becoming a nation of renters.

Whether we're talking about the predictable returns or high demand, we find apartment buildings to be inherently stable assets.

HIGH RISK-ADJUSTED RETURNS

A fundamental thesis of investing states that the riskier an investment, the higher the potential return should be. It makes sense. Nobody in their right mind would invest in something that has low expected returns coupled with high risk if there's a comparable investment opportunity offering the inverse (low risk, high return).

The purest embodiment of this dichotomy between risk and return are stocks and bonds. Stocks trend toward high risk, high return whereas bonds are the opposite, low risk with low return.

But here's the problem with this basic theory: it presumes an efficient marketplace filled with rational players.

Take a look around you at your bedfellows in the stock market. Do they seem particularly rational? Do *you* seem particularly rational?

Let's table that question for a moment and address the bogeyman in the corner: *risk.*

Every investment carries inherent risk. Unfortunately, despite our best efforts, in reality we don't actually have a great way of measuring risk. In fact, every investor has their own perception of what constitutes risk.

It could be relative to volatility or the probability of losing money. Then again, maybe it's the likelihood of losing *all* of your money.

Even if we all agreed on a universal definition of risk, it's simply not measurable, even with the gift of hindsight.

Most people mistakenly look back on history and assume that, just because a thing *did* happen, it was therefore *likely* to happen. But in a universe filled with infinite complexity, how can we ever even hope to calculate the probability of an event?

If we could do that with hindsight, then theoretically there would be nothing stopping us from accurately predicting events in the future. At that point it's simply a matter of computational power.

But I digress. Here's the point: we don't understand risk terribly well. For our purposes here, let's simplify and view it through the lens of volatility. Of course, past performance does not guarantee future performance, but we need a starting point whereby we can measure investment vehicles comparatively.

Through this lens, the question becomes: **Where does real estate fall on the risk-adjusted returns spectrum?**

First, to be clear, not all real estate is created equal. We're not interested in single-family homes, office space, or land, for example. Our focus, and the subject of this book, is multifamily apartment buildings.

This is an important distinction. Each of these niches has a different risk/return profile. Often, when people say, "Real estate is risky," they're referencing the 2008 financial crisis, which saw the single-family home sector get crushed.

Multifamily assets, by comparison, performed much better during the financial crisis than most people realize. While this sector definitely suffered from stagnant rent growth for a few years, overall, the default rate on multifamily assets during this period never rose above a single percentage point.

Let's return to the original question to figure out where exactly real estate falls on the risk-adjusted returns spectrum. Thankfully we have a marvelous twenty-year longitudinal study conducted by Thomson Reuters that offers a glimpse into the risk and return relationship between seven asset classes between the years 1993 and 2013. The graph below plots these different asset classes against risk and return.

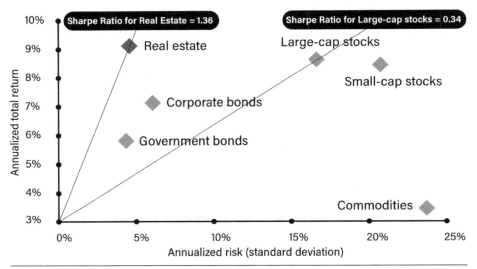

Source: Thomson Reuters Datastream. Data period: 3Q 1993 - 2Q 2013.
Indices used for each asset class: Government bonds = BofA Merrill Lynch Treasury Master, Corporate Bonds = Barclays U.S. Aggregate Corporate Intermediate, Core Real Estate = NCREIF Property Index (NPI), Large-cap Stocks = Russell 1000, Small-cap Stocks = Russell 2000, Commodities = S&P GSCI.

Stocks land in the upper right quadrant of the graph, indicating high average returns coupled with high risk. On the opposite side of the graph, government bonds occupy quadrant one with their promise of low returns and low risk.

So far, so good. Everything falls in line with conventional investing wisdom. That is, until we look in the upper left-hand quadrant, to that unicorn location of low risk and high return. There, we find the asset class of **commercial real estate**.

Take a moment to digest that. This twenty-year study revealed that commercial real estate (which includes multifamily, industrial, office, and retail) has returns equal to large-cap stocks, but a risk profile similar to government bonds.

While that's amazing, the study didn't even take into consideration the immense tax benefits associated with real estate investing. We'll address tax benefits in a later chapter. For now, it's enough to know that, once those benefits are factored in, the returns aren't even remotely close.

Regardless, the results are clear: commercial real estate blows stocks out of the water without any additional risk.

Here's the big question, given that these results seem to fly in the face of conventional investing wisdom: Why isn't everybody investing in commercial real estate rather than stocks?

Simply put, the general public lacks the education, experience, capital, and ability to meaningfully participate in this investment vehicle.

Now, think about how easily you can buy and sell stocks. You could open an account online and be trading on your phone within minutes. At work you were probably auto-enrolled in a 401(k) that invests directly in the stock market. It's ubiquitous for a reason.

That reason? Because there's a slew of people making incredible amounts of money when you invest in the stock market. They don't profit when you invest in real estate, so they're massively incentivized to keep your money on Wall Street, not Main Street.

If you're tired of hedge fund managers and brokers leeching off your returns, then maybe it's time to make a change.

Here's one last aspect of risk to consider: **inflation**.

As the amount of money in the system increases, the cost of goods and cost of living slowly rise to offset the weakening purchasing power of a single dollar. Put a pile of cash under your mattress and it'll lose value at a rate of about 2–5% per year. Multifamily real estate is a powerful inflationary hedge because we can raise rents to keep pace with inflation.

We effectively stop the devaluation of our money. How's that for risk management?

CONTROL

Recently the world experienced a massive shock: COVID-19. The pandemic rocked the stock market multiple times over the course of a year. Overnight, people witnessed their life savings plummet by over 20%. For the next twelve months, people watched as their retirement savings bounced up and down like a yo-yo.

If you held significant capital in the market, you might remember all the anxiety, futility, and powerlessness you felt.

During that same period of worldwide disruption, on the other hand, we made operational changes at our apartment buildings that immediately reduced expenses across all of our properties, mitigated vacancies, and ensured our multifamily assets continued performing.

Put simply: *we had control.*

Multifamily investing rewards skillful operators. It helps us sleep better at night knowing the ultimate success and failure of our investments rests in our hands, and not in the nameless, faceless hands of some corporate entity who might not have our best interests in mind.

And that's just what you get when you invest in the stock market: a senior management team that you have no connection to.

Knowing the operators you're investing with is one of the benefits of investing in a private real estate placement. When you have questions or concerns, you can simply call the sponsors to get an answer. Moving from investing in the faceless bureaucracy of Wall Street to the personal touch of Main Street is a great way to take control over your investing future.

CASH FLOW

Lest we paint a picture of pure rainbows and butterflies, let's point out that multifamily assets aren't without their downsides. Most notably, the issue of liquidity.

The stock market is incredibly liquid. Within minutes, you could pull out your phone and sell your entire portfolio. Easy. Then again, because it's so easy for you to sell, it's also easy for everybody else to sell. This, in a nutshell, gives birth to the stock market's inherent volatility.

Real estate, by comparison, is difficult to buy and sell. Despite real estate's illiquid nature, it offers something to offset this inconvenience: **cash flow.**

Cash flow is the profit remaining each month after expenses are deducted from top-line revenue. Investors receive this *profit* in the form of monthly or quarterly distributions, much like a dividend. This provides an ongoing stream of income to fund living expenses, a vacation, a pony, reinvestment, or whatever.

Best of all, the tax obligations of these distributions can, in many cases, be almost entirely deferred.

TAX BENEFITS

Let's talk about these mythical tax benefits.

But first, a disclaimer. We are not tax professionals in real life, nor do we play them on TV. Do not construe anything in these pages as tax or legal advice. You should speak to your tax and legal professionals about your unique situation before making any decisions that could affect your financial future.

Okay, you're sufficiently disclaimed. Let's move on.

Cash flow is amazing, but things get even better when we factor in the tax benefits. A couple quick takes on taxes:

First, the government doesn't want you overpaying. The purpose of the tax code is to outline all the ways to *reduce* your taxable liability. Seeking to legally reduce how much you pay in taxes isn't shady or illegal, it's smart, and it's exactly what all the wealthiest people (including our legislative representatives) utilize to keep more of what they earned.

Learn to use taxes to your advantage.

Second, the government offers tremendous perks to real estate investors because it's an important service they want to incentivize. And this makes sense. The government wants a strong economy and stable homes for its citizens.

The government doesn't want to take responsibility for housing people (which is a good thing, given the inefficiency of most government agencies), so they encourage investors to participate in this asset class by offering tax breaks, the most notable of which comes through the magic of *depreciation*.

Depreciation recognizes that buildings wear down over time and theoretically *lose* value. The government allows investors to write off this theoretical loss in value. Now, I say "theoretical" because, in reality, despite buildings wearing out, real estate tends to appreciate in value over time.

Why?

Because it's a finite resource (fixed supply) being competed over by an expanding population coupled with inflation (demand). All this leads to the double benefit of owning an asset that simultaneously appreciates *and* depreciates.

Pretty crazy, huh?

Unlike other investment vehicles, like stocks (which not only offer zero tax breaks, but are also taxed at unfavorable rates), this depreciation means you're unlikely to pay taxes on yearly cash flow over the life of a project.

That means more money in your pocket *now*. The **time value of money** and **opportunity cost** are powerful drivers of wealth when correctly utilized.

KEY CONCEPT

Time Value of Money
Here's a basic rule of investing: a dollar today is worth more than a dollar in the future, due to its potential earning capacity. If we have money sitting in a savings account, for instance, it's earning an interest rate and compounding.

Effectively, money in hand today can be put to work so that it's also earning.

Opportunity Cost
When we make a decision between two potential paths through life, we have to take into consideration the often-unseen effect of opportunity cost. What are those potential benefits we're foregoing by choosing one path over another?

Opportunity costs are often invisible and easily overlooked. That's a mistake.

The best decisions come after careful consideration of all the foreseeable opportunity costs. Failure to consider the opportunity costs results in a decision based on incomplete information.

The perfect investment vehicle?

Apartments aren't the perfect investment vehicle because there is no such thing. Every investment is inherently risky.

With that said, throughout all of our years of searching, we've yet to find any other investment vehicle that offers the same combination of stability, high risk-adjusted returns, control, cash flow, and tax benefits.

Most people, once they become aware of this investment vehicle, are eager to get involved, but they're faced with a couple potentially big hurdles to overcome.

First, money. Apartment buildings are expensive. There's no getting around that. Most people don't have enough money lying around to go out and buy a ten-million-dollar building.

Second, they lack the knowledge necessary to buy, operate, and sell a property.

The majority of people throw their hands up in despair and give up at this point. But not you. You're holding this book, which tells me you're committed to finding a way to overcome these obstacles.

Well, seek and ye shall find.

The answer is to partner with other investors in an apartment syndication.

CHAPTER 4

SYNDICATIONS

"Alone we can do so little; together we can do so much."

— Helen Keller

Success in real estate depends on your ability to purchase an asset at the right **price**, in the right **location**, with the right **team** executing the right **business plan**.

Most people don't have the time and energy, nor the desire, to gain the knowledge, research the markets, build the relationships, find the deals, or execute the business plan necessary to win in real estate.

You might be one of those people. You want to invest in real estate, but aren't interested in taking on a second job. That's where syndications come in.

Here's a simplified way of thinking about a syndication. We call it The

Jumbo Jet Investing Strategy.

Commercial flight is an incredible thing. Think about it: You could buy a plane ticket right now and be flying across the planet by the end of the day, sitting in a cozy seat watching a movie in an environment where the only decision you're expected to make is between the chicken or salad for dinner. And all of that occurs in a stress-free state of relaxation, even though you're hurtling across the globe at blistering speeds in a vehicle you probably know very little about.

Are you stressed? Perhaps at takeoff and landing, but unless you hit some turbulence, it's unlikely you'll worry too much about potentially crashing at any point throughout the flight.

That's the safety, convenience, and comfort we've come to expect from the jumbo jet.

In the world of real estate, the jumbo jet is a syndication. A group of investors pool their time, money, and knowledge to buy large properties that no single person in the group could have purchased or managed on their own.

Two types of investors participate in an apartment syndication: active and passive. The active investors are the **general partners** (a.k.a. the GP, sponsors, and operators) and they're responsible for all the things you probably think of when you think about buying real estate.

If we're sticking with the jumbo jet analogy, the GP is the group of experts making transcontinental flight possible. This experienced group of operators (similar to the pilots, flight attendants, ground control, and maintenance crew) leverage their unique skills and relationships to safely transport a group of passengers to their desired destination.

The passengers on this flight are the other group of investors: the **limited partners** (a.k.a. the LP or passive investors). They fund the deal by buying a ticket, and that's it.

Syndications bring active and passive investors together to fulfill the three core requirements of every deal: time, knowledge, and money. The general partners leverage their time and experience to identify viable markets, underwrite deals, secure bank financing, guarantee the loan, execute the business plan, handle investor relations, and oversee the exit of the asset. The limited partners, by contrast, simply bring the capital.

This synergy means the group can go further and faster together than any single investor could on their own.

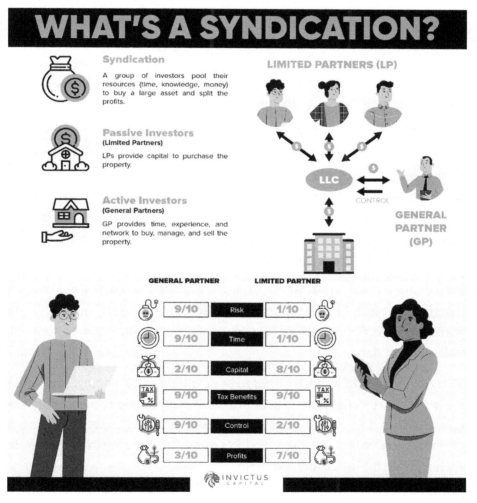

WHAT'S A SYNDICATION?

Syndication
A group of investors pool their resources (time, knowledge, money) to buy a large asset and split the profits.

Passive Investors
(Limited Partners)
LPs provide capital to purchase the property.

Active Investors
(General Partners)
GP provides time, experience, and network to buy, manage, and sell the property.

LIMITED PARTNERS (LP)

LLC

CONTROL

GENERAL PARTNER (GP)

GENERAL PARTNER		LIMITED PARTNER
9/10	Risk	1/10
9/10	Time	1/10
2/10	Capital	8/10
9/10	Tax Benefits	9/10
9/10	Control	2/10
3/10	Profits	7/10

INVICTUS CAPITAL

Something interesting to note about the syndication structure is that neither the limited partners nor the general partners actually *own* the piece of real estate being purchased—they own shares of the company that subsequently owns the real estate. It's a subtle yet important difference.

Within this structure, the general and limited partners have vastly different roles, responsibilities, and expectations.

Let's categorize these as risk, time, capital, tax benefits, control, and profits.

RISK

Remember, there is no such thing as a guaranteed return. Anybody selling a guarantee is selling a lie and breaking the law in the process. Every investment runs the risk of losing money. Let's assume that's the baseline level of risk for any investment.

This baseline is actually the maximum amount of risk the limited partners are exposed to within a syndication. Even if everything goes sideways, the passive investors bear no real possibility of losing more than their initial investment (except in the case of a capital call whereby you might elect to put more money into a struggling deal to help it find traction). The general partners, by comparison, carry a much higher degree of risk.

Pretty much every apartment syndication relies on bank financing to purchase an asset. These loans are typically for between 60 and 80% of the purchase price. On a multi-million-dollar property, that equals a substantial chunk of debt.

Many Americans have been raised to believe debt is the enemy. And while it's true that certain types of debt are to be avoided, we're personally big fans of using debt to purchase cash-flow-generating assets. Debt used in this way is called leverage, and it's one of the reasons real estate is such a powerful investment vehicle.

The debt used to acquire a property falls into one of two categories: recourse or non-recourse.

A non-recourse loan is only secured by the collateral (i.e. the property) itself. If the borrower defaults, the bank can take back the building, but that's it. The operators aren't personally liable for the remainder of the loan.

A recourse loan, on the other hand, has no such protections. If the borrower defaults, the bank could come after the loan guarantor's personal assets, including income, other properties, or savings.

In either case, the limited partner bears no liability in the eyes of the bank. Even if the deal goes completely south, the bank can't come after the limited partner.

Also, syndications are tightly regulated by the SEC, and grossly negligent operators could easily find themselves on the wrong side of a civil lawsuit from their investors seeking restitutions.

All told, the general partners carry significantly more risk than the limited partners. This doesn't guarantee results, but it does create an environment where the sponsors are strongly incentivized to effectively execute the business plan.

TIME

Limited partners have three jobs in an apartment syndication:

1. Find a general partner
2. Analyze opportunities
3. Fund deals

Of these three tasks, it's the first one that requires the most time and energy. Oh yeah, and it's also the limited partner's most important job.

Why?

Because great operators will turn lemons into lemonade. A bad operator will take lemonade and just spill it all over the floor.

Initially, the vetting process will take you the most time and energy. But once you've located a fantastic operator, the amount of time spent vetting future investment opportunities diminishes. That's the speed of trust.

After a deal closes, all that remains for you to do is open a monthly/quarterly email and hop on the occasional call or webinar with the general partners to keep your finger on the pulse of the project. No fielding angry tenant phone calls in the middle of the night, negotiating with contractors, or making sure all the bills get paid on time.

Sounds kind of awesome, huh?

CAPITAL

Remember the three things every deal requires?

Time, Knowledge, Money

If the general partners bring the time and knowledge, then that leaves the limited partners to bring the majority of the capital.

In most deals, the general partners co-invest alongside the LPs. After all, if it's a great deal, why wouldn't they? Even so, the limited partners typically account for over 80% of the raised capital.

TAX BENEFITS

I would remind you that I'm not a tax professional and this shouldn't be construed as tax advice. Speak to your tax adviser before making any decisions that could impact your current financial position.

With that said, there are a lot of reasons to love real estate investing. One of our favorites (and one of the most overlooked) are the tax benefits. The benefits garnered through depreciation are incredible.

We'll cover taxes in much more detail later.

CONTROL

At first glance, the limited partner's lack of control might seem like a bad thing, but upon closer inspection, it's not.

Operating a multifamily asset is hard. Skillful execution is rewarded, unlike in many other investment vehicles. The beauty of a syndication is that it allows you to partner with world-class operators and benefit from their years of experience and ability.

This isn't like small residential properties, where it doesn't matter how well you run the asset. Once you step into big apartment buildings, the game changes and you're now in the big leagues with a higher level of competition and standard of play. For you to gain a similar level of competency would take years of hard work and effort, which, since you're reading a book on passive investing, I'm guessing isn't what you're looking for.

That's all right, the symbiotic relationship between general partner and limited partner means both sides come out further ahead working together than they would by working alone.

Now, many first-time passive investors are put off by the fact that they have very little voting power or control in what happens with an apartment syndication. But this is actually a good thing.

Similar to the pilot of the jumbo, you want professionals in control, making decisions *they* think are in the best interests of the investment.

If the limited partners have too much say in key decisions, then suddenly a slew of other passengers (many of whom have little practical real estate knowledge) are in the cockpit offering their two cents on important decisions that directly impact *your* investment. To avoid this, you want the general partners retaining majority of control over the project.

PROFITS

We'll cover the topic of profits in minute detail later. It's a critical topic that can get quite convoluted. For our purposes here, we'll keep things relatively basic to provide a high-level overview.

The most common equity split in an apartment syndication falls somewhere around 70/30, meaning 70% of the equity goes to the limited partners and 30% goes to the general partners. There are countless equity structures, and some get quite convoluted. In most deals, the limited partners are entitled to the majority of the profits.

It's not uncommon to double your money in only three to five years in an apartment syndication. Good luck beating those returns in the stock market.

But now that you understand apartment syndications from a high level, it's time to make a decision every new investor must answer: **Do you want to be an active or a passive investor?**

This book makes the assumption you want to passively invest, but you might still be straddling the proverbial fence between these two camps. Before we go any further, it's time to decide which side of the fence you want to call home.

CHAPTER 5

DECIDING WHAT KIND OF INVESTOR YOU WANT TO BE

"If you do not know where you come from, then you don't know where you are, and if you don't know where you are, then you don't know where you're going. And if you don't know where you're going, you're probably going wrong."

— Sir Terry Pratchett

The call came at 2 a.m. one month after closing my first property. Bleary-eyed and half asleep, I stared at the name flashing across my phone's screen. It was one of my new tenants.

This can't be good, I thought.

"You need to get over here," the tenant said. "A SWAT team is about to break down the neighbor's door."

I shook the cobwebs from my sleep-addled brain and tried piecing together the man's words. *Wait... did he just say "SWAT"?*

I pulled back the blinds covering the window, expecting to see the blue-and-red lights of police squad cars surrounding *my* home. Thankfully, all I could see was a good old-fashioned Minnesota blizzard.

My tenant put an officer on the phone and he rattled off words at a million miles a minute. I only managed to catch roughly 23% of them, and of the words I did catch, most didn't sound good: "fugitive," "felon," "drugs," "warrant"...

The officer told me we could avoid the hassle of kicking down any doors if I got over there quickly. I don't like replacing doors, but did I mention that blizzard? Because that was a problem.

I drive a Prius C (which is the tiny Prius, for those who care about these kinds of things). It's a wee little car known for its ability to drive a million miles per gallon... less well known for its clearance or traction.

Still, this is the life of a landlord, so my girlfriend and I jumped into the car and braved the weather. A trip that usually took twenty minutes stretched into a full hour, every ten minutes of which I received another frantic call from my tenant reminding me that the police were polishing their door-kicking-in boots.

I was white-knuckling the steering wheel, trying my best to keep us on the road, and my girlfriend suggested we call the police department to see if they could provide any additional information.

Many memorable mistakes in my life can be tracked back to not listening to my significant other. I grunted something dismissive and plowed ahead. Sometimes that's just what happens when you're in panic-stricken crisis mode.

We pulled up to the property to find a man standing in the middle of the road in shin-high snow. He was garbed in full tactical gear from the local Army surplus store and, if that wasn't crazy enough, this man then leapt in front of an oncoming car, gun and flashlight waving wildly. The panicked driver slammed on the brakes, 'cause stopping seemed better than involuntary vehicular manslaughter.

The gun-toting madman ordered that driver out of their car and of course they complied, because what else are you really going to do in that situation? That was the moment I realized these weren't police officers. I would later learn that these were, in fact, bounty hunters.

When the guy with the shotgun strapped to his chest turned to me next, I also did as he requested, because I'm not in the business of being disagreeable to crazy people with guns. Let me just tell you, in case you're wondering, that none of the "How to Invest in Real Estate" books adequately prepare you to handle bounty hunters.

To this day, that was my longest night as a landlord and in the end, it was a whole lot of hullaballoo that amounted to nothing. After a thorough check of the building, the bounty hunters failed to find their target and eventually gave up. They disappeared into the blizzardy-night, never to be seen nor heard from again

I share this story because at some point most new investors debate whether they should be an active or a passive investor in real estate. There's no one-size-fits-all answer to this question, unfortunately, but here are a few factors to consider:

1. **Your Personality:** Do you like being in control and hands-on?
2. **Your Availability:** Do you have the time to manage an active portfolio?
3. **Your Experience:** Do you know enough to effectively operate a multi-family asset?
4. **Your Investment Goals:** Do you want an investment or a job?

That last point is worth repeating. ***What are your investment goals?***

Are you seeking a steady stream of cash flow checks delivering solid yearly returns with little to no effort? Are you tired of your W-2 job and want to make a switch that fast-tracks your financial journey? Do you enjoy the rush of closing a deal and live for that squirt of dopamine each time you flip a house?

There are many great ways to invest in real estate and each one is effective when executed correctly. The question, "Should I passively invest in a syndication or should I go out and buy my own property?" can really only be answered from the perspective of *your* unique situation.

We can't make the decision for you, but we've worked with hundreds of passive investors, and here are four of the reasons they chose the passive route.

Note: Not having to deal with bounty hunters in the middle of the night didn't make the list, but it should go without saying.

1. Limited Risk

We've already discussed multifamily investing risk through the lens of stability. Here's another aspect to consider. In an apartment syndication, the limited partners don't sign on the loan.

"Limited" is the key word in "limited partner." In exchange for giving up operational control over the asset, you bear no liability should something go wrong with the property and the bank foreclose. A limited partner's risk in a syndication generally extends no further than possibly losing their initial capital (an inherent risk in any investment). Knowing the bank won't come after my personal assets if something goes wrong certainly helps me sleep better at night.

2. Operator Expertise

Our mission at Invictus Capital is to reduce the complexity of multifamily investing so more people can participate in this powerful asset class.

The beauty of multifamily investing lies in its simplicity. By the end of this book, in fact, you'll have a pretty firm understanding of the whole business model.

But it's a mistake to equate *simple* with *easy*. The fundamentals of this industry are straightforward and relatively simple. Most adults can easily understand the systems and economic drivers underpinning a quality investment within a reasonable amount of time. Executing those systems, however, is more difficult than the social media gurus would have you believe.

Apartment investing is a lot like bench-pressing an alligator. Simple in concept, difficult in practice.

That's not to say some asset classes within real estate aren't easier than others. Buying and operating a single-family home is much easier than buying and operating a 200-unit apartment complex. Then again, the large multifamily apartment complex generally has a better risk-to-return profile than a single-family home.

So why not go out and buy your own apartment building? Because the stakes are quite high in large multifamily assets. Mistakes can be dire.

If you want to succeed, you must partner with top-notch operators. The magnitude of the systems, capital, and potential issues at play means an operator's skill plays a huge role in the outcome of an asset's performance.

That's less the case in the single-family space, where the difference between a mom-and-pop owner and a world-class operator doesn't move the needle very much. These smaller properties are valued based on comparables, which don't take into consideration how well or poorly an asset's being run.

If you're considering actively managing a multifamily asset, then consider the following question: **Do you have the time, energy, and desire to gain the knowledge, experience, and relationships necessary**

to succeed?

The answer to that question will ultimately determine the trajectory of your overall investing career.

3. Alignment of Interest

"Show me the incentive and I will show you the outcome."

— Charlie Munger

Whenever you're relying on a third party to realize an objective on your behalf, there exists an inherent friction between you and them. Welcome to the principal-agent problem. It occurs because what you (the principal) want and what the other party (the agent) wants are rarely in perfect alignment.

For instance, investors want to realize strong returns without incurring excessive risk. However, if your investment manager's compensation is tied to achieving above-average returns, then they're encouraged to pursue opportunities capable of producing those results while disregarding the downside.

This relationship is particularly pronounced where property managers are concerned. If you're buying small residential properties and you don't have the time or desire to field tenant phone calls in the middle of the night, you'll hire a third-party property management company to run the day-to-day operations.

Zooming out a bit, you'll realize that the sponsors of an apartment syndication are similar to those third-party property managers. The key difference lies in the magnitude of returns at stake and how those returns are realized through the ownership structure.

Third-party property management companies typically charge flat fees, which only ever earn them a couple thousand dollars at a time. The margins aren't great, so they survive through scale.

This creates two problems:

1. Are they giving your property the attention it deserves, or do they cut corners to provide marginal service across their entire portfolio?
2. With thin margins, will your property manager be tempted to gouge on fees?

Contrast this with how deal sponsors in a syndication are compensated.

Deal sponsors also collect fees (which we'll break down in greater detail later) for the work that went into acquiring or managing the asset. In both cases, fees are nice, but they don't amount to life-changing sums of money for the sponsors.

The majority of a sponsor's compensation should be tied to their share of equity in a project. Depending on the deal, a sponsor could make millions of dollars upon the successful sale of the property.

With so much at stake, it's unlikely (though not impossible) that the sponsor will skim a little off the top here and there. It's not only the magnitude of returns that keeps sponsors honest, though. It's also the fact that the future of their business depends on their ability to deliver on investor expectations.

Happy investors are not only returning investors, but they're also likely to refer friends and family on future opportunities. Reputation is everything. Operators who fail to deliver don't stay in business very long.

These distinctions mean the sponsors are far more in alignment with their investor's long-term goals than the property management team hired to run your portfolio of single-family homes.

4. Geographic and Asset Class Diversification

Passively investing in an apartment syndication doesn't limit you to a single market or asset class in the same way investing actively does. Take Invictus Capital, for example: we're vertically integrated, which means we have an in-house property management team.

We have extreme control over our operational expenses because it's our own boots on the ground. The downside is that we're limited in the markets we can pursue. Our infrastructure works best and realizes powerful synergies when we group our assets in relatively close proximity to one another. We can't just pick up and move to the newest hot market.

Let's go another layer deeper and consider our expertise as multifamily operators. We focus exclusively on multifamily assets. We're not self-storage or mobile home park professionals. We're hyper-focused on our asset class because that's where we have a competitive advantage. This limits our ability to diversify, however. We can't easily hop between asset classes.

Passive investors don't face either of these limitations. Because passive investors aren't tied to a physical location or a certain asset class, they have greater flexibility in pursuing alternative markets, operators, and investment vehicles.

If there's a smoking hot deal in North Carolina for a 182-mobile home park community, great! Assuming you have confidence in the team, the market, the asset class, and the business plan, there's nothing stopping you from putting your money to work.

Optionality is important, especially in the state of the current market, where killer deals are few and far between. When you're limited to a single market, there's a ceiling on how many deals a single operator can generate within a certain period of time.

None of this means you *have* to diversify into other markets, operators, or asset classes, but it's nice to know you *can*.

SHOULD YOU PASSIVELY INVEST?

How you answer this question depends upon your goals and desired end state.

If you like the idea of rolling up your sleeves and putting in the hard work to grow and operate an active real estate portfolio, then you should pursue that goal with focus and determination. If you do, we're confident you'll find success.

Then again, if you're drawn to the idea of reaping above-average returns with an incredible risk profile *without* having to put in long hours of work, then passive investing in apartment syndications might be the best option for you.

Either way, the only wrong choice is to do neither.

Far too many people have embarked on an investing journey without ever stopping to consider their desired destination or how they intend to get there.

Granted, they might have some loose conception of where they're going, but when it comes to you and your family's financial well-being, a "loose conception" isn't good enough. You must know with absolute clarity where you're going and which roads will get you there.

Unfortunately, most of us have lived our entire lives feeling either terrified or overwhelmed when we think about our finances. And it's not necessarily our fault. Financial literacy wasn't covered in school, and most of us didn't grow up in households that openly discussed financial matters. Not only that, but there's a cultural taboo against talking about money with friends, family, or even strangers.

Which is ridiculous. How are we supposed to learn or improve our financial situations if everybody simply sticks their heads in the sand?

To add salt to this perfect recipe for disaster, consider the fact that the financial institutions (banks, hedge fund managers, financial advisers, etc.) have dressed the whole industry in a veneer of complexity designed specifically to make us feel overwhelmed.

Why would they do that? Because it keeps them in work.

If the general population feels it's beyond their ability to take control of their financial futures, then it makes sense that they'd outsource the responsibility to a professional.

We use the term "professional" loosely here. Recall the sage advice, "Don't take advice from anybody who you wouldn't swap places with." Most financial advisers are not wealthy. And while hedge fund managers and stockbrokers *might* be, it's not from following the advice they're giving *you*.

No, they make their money *off* of you. Or, rather, at your expense.

Now, we're not suggesting you kick your financial adviser to the curb. Instead, we want you behind the wheel, captaining the ship of your financial destiny. The first step is to decide where you want to go and then decide how you want to get there.

A young professional, fresh out of college with years of runway ahead of them, might take a different path than someone in their mid-thirties or forties with a couple kids and an established career. And both of these will make decisions that look different than those made by somebody in their sixties closing in on retirement.

In the first instance, the young buck might be comfortable investing in higher-risk projects because they're seeking to maximize the velocity of their capital. With the benefit of a long runway before retirement, they can withstand short-term bumps in the road. They have the most precious of resources available, time. And with that, they can delay gratification and seek big appreciation plays.

Our investor in their mid-thirties with a family might have completely different goals. That person's biggest objective might be to create additional streams of passive income to offset their W-2 paycheck so they can spend more time with their family. This investor has one eye toward the future and the other on the *present*. A child only takes their first step once, after all. You're either there to see it or you're not.

With this in mind, these investors might seek projects offering decent appreciation potential coupled with strong cash flow to supplement their lifestyle *now*.

And all of this might change once you're within spitting distance of retirement. Here, you're no longer interested in getting the most bang for your buck. Now it's all about capital preservation.

There are few things a soon-to-be retiree wants to see less than the stock market tanking by 20% mere months before or after their retirement. Savvy investors find solid, inflation-hedged investments in real assets that they're confident won't blow up their life savings in an instant.

These three scenarios are pulled from an infinite multitude that fall all along the risk-return spectrum. In a later chapter, we'll discuss which investment vehicles might best serve these respective investors, but for now simply realize the importance of knowing your personal investment parameters, along with your temperament, from the very beginning.

Before we move on, that last bit merits repeating. *Your temperament matters.*

Some people are naturally more risk-averse than others. Where your tolerance for risk falls on the spectrum will dictate what sorts of investment opportunities you pursue.

At the end of the day, how you make your money matters. If you've taken on more risk than your subconscious mind can handle, you're going to have a stressful go of it. Say hello to sleepless nights.

Now, be honest with yourself. Everybody likes to think they'll have ice water in their veins when the chips are down, but most people don't. Furthermore, who wants ice in their veins?!

I don't know about you, but I'm not looking for excitement when it comes to my investments. If my adrenaline gets pumping when thinking about an opportunity, it's usually a sign that I need to slow down and take a deep breath.

There's a thin line between investing and speculating. Usually you know you've crossed that line when emotions get involved.

At the end of the day, many paths will take you to your desired end state. Take the time to reflect on your personality and goals so that you can pursue the path that's right for you. Once you're clear on this, it's time to move on to the next step in the process: finding opportunities that match your parameters.

CHAPTER 6

THE PARTNERS

ACCREDITED VERSUS NON-ACCREDITED INVESTORS

Here's something that seems counterintuitive at first glance: When you invest in an apartment syndication, you're not actually buying a piece of real estate. You're buying shares of the LLC (or company) that ultimately owns the property.

Also, because you're passively participating with the expectation of earning profit, these deals are regulated by the Securities and Exchange Commission (SEC).

This is great for passive investors. It creates multiple layers of additional protection for your investment. It also, however, creates more paperwork, expenses, and a few more hoops for the deal sponsor to jump through.

Thankfully, the SEC doesn't require sponsors to fully register their offerings, which would simply be cost-prohibitive for these investments. Instead, we're able to file exemptions in a couple different ways, the most

PASSIVE INVESTING MADE SIMPLE

common taking place under Rules 506(b) and 506(c).

So what's the difference between these two rules, and why should you care?

Well, to answer that, you have to first understand whether you're an **accredited investor**.

There are many ways to qualify as an accredited investor, but here are the two most common:

1. You made at least $200,000 of annual income in the previous two years ($300,000 for a married couple), or,
2. You have a net worth in excess of $1,000,000 (excluding the value of your primary residence).

If you look at those requirements and think that they pose a pretty high barrier to entry, then you're right. Only about 10% of the American population are accredited investors.

Why should your income or net worth matter?

Agree with it or not, the SEC believes these individuals are more capable of accepting the economic risks associated with investing in unregistered securities. To put it another way, they can afford to lose the money. Also, simply because they *have* money, the SEC assumes they're knowledgeable and savvy investors. Talk about poor logic.

This leads us to Rule 506(c). Because this rule only allows accredited investors to participate, deal sponsors can publicly advertise their offerings on social media, a billboard, podcasts, or wherever. That's great if you're an accredited investor, because you have access to a whole slew of passive investment opportunities.

The downside is that investors must verify their accredited status, and simply checking a box on a form isn't good enough. A third-party verification service is usually involved, which creates a headache most accredited investors simply don't want to deal with.

Now, if you're part of the 90% who don't qualify as an accredited investor, you might be wondering if you've wasted your time reading this far. No, you sure haven't. Rule 506(b) swoops in to save the day!

Most private real estate placements utilize Rule 506(b) because it allows "sophisticated" investors to participate in these offerings. In 2019 alone, over $36 billion was raised through private placement apartment syndications. Of these, 85% utilized Rule 506(b).

A "sophisticated" investor has sufficient knowledge and experience in financial and business matters to evaluate the risk and merits of a prospective investment. By reading this book, you're becoming more sophisticated. Huzzah!

Now, for the limitations.

First, 506(b) allows for only thirty-five non-accredited investors and an unlimited number of accredited investors to participate in an offering.

Second, and most important for our purposes, syndicators cannot publicly advertise their offerings. That's right, no social media, television, billboards. Heck, when utilizing this exemption, you're not even allowed to talk about the deal in public.

Only the non-accredited investors who have a substantive preexisting relationship with the deal sponsor can participate in these offerings.

What qualifies as a substantive relationship? For starters, it means the deal sponsor has sufficient information about your financial circumstances and level of investing sophistication to decide whether you qualify as a "sophisticated investor."

Okay, what about that "preexisting" part? Unfortunately, the SEC hasn't offered much guidance on that front. They've kept things intentionally vague.

Could you meet a deal sponsor today, wait a week, and then see a deal from them? Probably not.

Operators usually enforce a one month "cooling-off" period before they start presenting deals to a potential non-accredited investor.

This means, if you're a sophisticated investor, you need to do two things before you can participate in a syndication:

1. Educate yourself
2. Build relationships with syndicators

CREATING A SUBSTANTIVE RELATIONSHIP

We're big fans of staying on the right side of the SEC. Unfortunately, that's not the default mindset of operators in an industry so small that plenty of unscrupulous sponsors simply gamble on the fact that the SEC will never catch wind of their wrongdoings.

Maybe they're right, but here's the thing: rules are never a problem when things are going well. When investors get their projected returns and everything ticks along according to plan, nobody tends to stand up and rock the boat.

But what happens when things go south and a deal fails to perform as expected? You can bet the first call a disgruntled limited partner will make is to their attorney, searching for a way out of the deal.

Operators who weren't sufficiently diligent in establishing a preexisting relationship stand to get buried under a mountain of sawdust from all the corners they cut.

Besides, operators lax in complying with SEC requirements are surely lax in other areas. These aren't the types of partners you want to work with.

If only these guys and gals wore a badge with skulls on it to show that they are, in fact, the bad guys, like they do in the movies. Unfortunately, in real life it's much harder to know who you can trust.

Assuming the deal sponsor you've selected is on the up-and-up, here's a sample workflow you could expect before they allow you to participate in their 506(b) offering.

1. **Sponsor Publicly Advertises Company:** Companies can advertise themselves and their services, but not a specific deal. Our approach at Invictus Capital focuses on producing educational content that delivers huge value. Once people understand this amazing investment vehicle, it practically sells itself.

2. **Investor Application:** Here you'll signal your intent to receive future deal-specific communications, often through an online application. Most forms ask a few qualifying questions to assess where you are in your investor journey so that the operator understands your goals, knowledge, and capacity and can appropriately pair you with the right opportunity.

3. **Introductory Phone Call:** This call establishes the beginning of your relationship, and it's critical. Think of it like a first date. This conversation provides an opportunity for you to get to know the operator and vice versa. At this point, you're still not discussing specific deals. Instead, you're sharing information about your past, experience level, and financial position, while also grilling the operator on their process, investment philosophy, and track record.

4. **Cooling-Off Period:** After your initial call, it's time to cool your jets. The *cooling-off period* establishes a substantial enough preexisting relationship before you can be presented a deal. Expect a cooling-off period of around thirty days. That's not to say that you can't have ongoing conversations or interactions with the operator during this period. In fact, you should. At this point, you should be on their email list and receiving regular communications. Use this information to deepen your understanding of the operator, who they are, how they

communicate, and whether they are somebody you could work with.

5. **Deal Presentation:** Finally, once you're sufficiently cooled, you're welcomed into the hallowed halls of private placements and can start receiving deals from the operator.

You've jumped through a lot of hoops, but it's for your own safety and security. The SEC's goal is to protect the general population from unscrupulous operators and questionable investment opportunities.

Because they allow apartment syndicators to bypass the lengthy and expensive registration process, we have to follow these extra guidelines to ensure investors aren't blindly walking into a bad deal with a silver-tongued rascal.

ROLES AND RESPONSIBILITIES OF THE GENERAL PARTNERSHIP

Every deal needs three things: time, knowledge, and capital.

From a high level, it's fairly accurate to say that the limited partners bring the capital and that's it. Everything else falls under the purview of the general partners.

There's a lot of moving parts in an apartment syndication, and it's unlikely any single individual could effectively manage them all. Most deal sponsor teams are typically comprised of a few members. There's no limit to the number of people who *could* be part of the general partnership, but it's rare to see much more than five to seven people. Beyond that, and you have to start wondering what unique value the additional team members bring to the party.

Although the engine powering a syndication forward is somewhat complex, all the roles and responsibilities of the general partners can be distilled into one of four buckets:

1. Acquisition
2. Capital raising
3. Loan guarantor
4. Asset management

Let's break these down so you have a basic understanding of what goes into each role.

ACQUISITION

Much of the work involved in closing a property is completely invisible to the limited partners.

Behind every successful closing there exists months, if not years, spent building relationships with brokers, lenders, and potential sellers. For every one deal closed, a hundred potential opportunities were probably underwritten, twenty-five opportunities toured, and ten offers submitted.

Once a property goes under contract, the deal sponsor must now provide the **risk capital**. This money could potentially be lost if the deal falls apart and it includes the earnest money (often 0.5–1% of purchase price), fees associated with preparing the legal paperwork, and the cost of conducting due diligence on the property (hiring engineers, architects, plumbers, electricians, etc.).

During this period, the acquisition team arranges financing through the bank while also coordinating the closing dates with the title company and seller.

Simply put, an immense amount of time and energy goes into any deal that eventually makes it to a passive investor's desk.

CAPITAL RAISING

The amount of capital a team can raise directly impacts the size and quantity of deals they can execute. Operators ensure they have sufficient capital flow in a couple different ways.

First, they split their focus between operating preexisting deals, finding new deals, and raising capital. On any given day, these operators could run from one meeting discussing a potential acquisition with a broker to a phone call with an interested investor. After that, they might find themselves in a discussion with the property management team to discuss the portfolio's current performance for the month.

Juggling all these balls is difficult, which is why some sponsors ensure sufficient capital flow by partnering directly with groups who *exclusively* focus on raising capital.

These capital-raising partners focus primarily on investor relations, networking with worthy operators, and vetting deals presented to them by sponsors who will focus on the operation and acquisition of an asset.

As a passive investor, you may enjoy working with capital raisers because it saves you from vetting countless operators. You find the capital raiser and the capital raiser does the work of vetting potential partners. When a deal comes, the *capital raiser* puts it through their underwriting filter and, if it passes, they present it to you.

The extra set of eyeballs on a project, plus the fact that capital raisers are probably better at vetting deals and partnerships than you, means you're that much less likely to jump into a bad opportunity.

At least, that's the theory.

LOAN GUARANTOR / KEY PRINCIPAL (KP)

Depending on the type of loan utilized, the bank might impose some high lending requirements of the general partnership. Most often, they want to see that the sponsors have a net worth equal to the size of the loan while maintaining a certain amount of liquidity.

This makes sense. If they're going to lend a couple million dollars, they want to know that the deal sponsors have sufficient financial where-withal to ride out any potential rough patches. Failing that, if things go completely sideways on a deal, they want some means for recouping their losses through the loan guarantor's personal assets.

When we're talking about purchasing properties worth tens of millions of dollars, these requirements become quite prohibitive. In these instances, the deal sponsor will usually bring on a high-net-worth individual (i.e. a key principal or balance sheet partner) to sign on the loan in exchange for a fee or percentage of the general partnership.

ASSET MANAGEMENT

The asset manager oversees the project throughout the life of the hold. This includes managing the successful execution of the business plan, filing all relevant tax and legal documents on time (investor K-1s, for instance), and handling ongoing investor communications.

Don't confuse asset management with property management, by the way.

The asset manager works closely with the property management team to set direction and hold accountability. They'll usually meet at least once a week to check in on key performance indicators and to make high-level decisions about the operation of the asset. Asset management is critical, so get crystal clear on who exactly sits in this seat and their relevant experience.

The property management team, on the other hand, are the actual boots-on-the-grounds meeting with prospective tenants, signing leases, and executing unit turns.

All right, now that we understand the basic partnership structure of an

apartment syndication, let's turn our focus to the two tangible benefits every investor expects when investing in real estate: returns and
tax benefits.

CHAPTER 7

RETURNS AND TAXES

RETURNS

"Price is what you pay. Value is what you get."

— Warren Buffett

Buckle up, 'cause we're about to get technical to discuss the nuts and bolts of how exactly you get paid in an apartment syndication.

Before we can do that, however, we have to zoom out to get a bird's-eye view of the investment structure to understand how returns get paid out. There's an infinite number of ways one could structure an investment, so this is no small task.

But that's okay, because by the end of this chapter you'll understand all the individual pieces of the puzzle and how they fit together. With that knowledge, you should be able to make sense of most offerings.

With that said, there are some truly convoluted return structures. Recently, in fact, an offering came across our desk that made our heads absolutely spin. We're professionals, and even *we* couldn't make heads or tails of it.

This usually happens for one of two reasons:

1. The deal sponsor is new and inexperienced.
2. The deal sponsor is trying too hard to make the numbers work.

Be careful on both fronts.

We're simple guys and prefer deals structured in simple, straightforward ways. We want our passive investors to understand what's happening without requiring an advanced degree in mathematics.

If you find yourself wading into an offering and continually getting lost in the convoluted structure, that might be a sign that that deal isn't right for you.

All right, to understand investment structures and returns, we must first understand a little thing called the capital stack.

THE CAPITAL STACK

The capital stack determines who gets paid and in what order.

If we stack all the capital utilized to finance a piece of real estate, the lowest risk instrument lives on the bottom. This is the senior debt, and it's the foundation of the capital stack. On the other end, common equity sits atop the capital stack in the highest risk position. The capital stack, in its simplest form, might only consist of these two blocks.

Most often, the bank claims the senior debt position. It's considered the lowest risk position because senior debt is collateralized by the asset itself. In the case of default, the senior debt holder can lay claim to the property.

Because senior debt carries such low risk by comparison to the rest of the stack, it also commands the lowest returns. Senior debt holders don't benefit from the potential upside of a deal. The debt investor receives the same return regardless of whether the deal is a grand slam or just a base hit.

Common equity holders get paid last, if at all, and by consequence carry the most risk. If a project fails, equity holders stand to lose their principal investment when the senior debt holder forecloses on the asset. In exchange for the increased risk, equity holders stand to gain the most if the project is a roaring success.

The hybrid instruments of mezzanine debt and preferred equity occasionally sit between senior debt and common equity.

Mezzanine debt sits subordinate to senior debt and carries limited foreclosure rights. To offset this lack of security, mezzanine debt holders require higher returns than the senior debt holders.

Senior debt most often comes from a bank. Mezzanine debt, on the other hand, can come through another bank (willing to take a subordinate position) or through individual investors.

These debt investors sit in a better, more low-risk position in the capital stack than equity investors do. Sometimes mezzanine debt holders also participate in some of the profits at sale. Risk-averse investors seeking a solid yield or a hedge against inflation love this structure.

One last hybrid instrument sits between a pure debt or equity investment, and it's called **preferred equity**.

Preferred equity is an interesting instrument, bridging the gap between debt and equity. It shares an ownership interest in the company itself (like a common equity holder), but it pays a fixed dividend.

You could think of it like a pseudo-bond and you wouldn't be entirely off-base.

Preferred equity holders enjoy solid returns a notch or two below those of the common equity holders. To offset these lower returns, preferred equity holders benefit from getting paid out first.

Depending on the deal structure, preferred equity holders may participate in the proceeds of a sale above and beyond their fixed coupon.

There's a place in the capital stack for you regardless of your investing parameters. Just understand exactly where you sit in the stack.

If you're a common equity holder, for instance, recognize that you get paid last. If there's a long line of investors sitting in front of you in the mezzanine debt and preferred equity positions, then this may drastically influence your payout schedule, depending on how well (or poorly) a project performs.

Which position is right for you?

Well, first, not all deals will offer the full buffet of options. Most apartment syndications we've seen only offer a common equity position (although preferred equity positions have become increasingly common in recent years).

If you're drawn to the security afforded by debt investing, then you'll need to find a particular subset of operators to work with. This is why it's so important to set your investment parameters from the outset.

RETURNS

The Equity Split

So, who exactly gets what?

There are countless ways to structure the equity split of a syndication. Honestly, they can get pretty complicated once you start factoring in waterfalls, hurdles, and catch-ups. Let's keep things simple and distill the equity split down to its most basic form.

Most deals have an equity split around 70/30, with the limited partners owning 70% of the project and the general partners owning the remaining 30%. Again, these numbers vary depending on the operator, their track record, the strength of the deal, and myriad other factors, but this is a good starting point.

Let's pretend we have a screaming good deal and raise $1,000,000 to purchase a building for $2,000,000 and are offering a 70/30 split. In the first year, the property spits out a nice 10% cash-on-cash return (don't worry, we'll cover return metrics and how they're calculated in a later chapter), creating $100,000 worth of cash flow to be distributed to all the members. With our 70/30 split, $70,000 of that goes to the limited partners and $30,000 goes to the general partners.

Now, if you'd invested $100,000 and purchased 10% of the limited partnership ($100,000/$1,000,000), you would receive 10% of that $70,000 for a distribution of $7,000 (and a cash-on-cash return of 7%).

This example is simple by design to outline the basic structure of an equity split. Things only get more complicated from here, but don't worry, we'll build our understanding layer by layer and by the end you'll have a rock-solid framework for evaluating deal structures.

Ultimately, the precise equity split ratios don't matter. Whether the deal offers a 90/10 or a 50/50 split is irrelevant, assuming the deal delivers projected returns in alignment with your investing goals. If your investment criteria requires a 10% cash-on-cash return with a 15% IRR over a five-year hold, and the 50/50 split nails that... great!

If the deal projects to come in under those minimum numbers, then regardless of how favorable the split appears, it's not the right deal for you.

Now that we've laid the bedrock and you have a foundational understanding of the equity split, let's fill out this framework with some more detail and discuss the different points at which you'll get paid in a syndication.

CASH FLOW DISTRIBUTIONS

Cash flow distributions are the most regular payment you'll receive. Cash flow is the profit left over each month after all expenses are deducted from revenue, and it's the lifeblood of a healthy investment.

At the most fundamental level, cash flow implies the property generates a surplus of cash after covering all its expenses, which means the asset is functionally self-supporting. These distributions put money in your pocket now, which can be used to pay bills, offset W-2 income, or fund future investment opportunities.

CAPITAL EVENT

Cash flow makes you rich. Appreciation makes you wealthy.

There's a lot of truth to that saying. Typically, the most substantial gains are realized when one of two capital events occur: a sale or a refinance. An asset might generate tens of thousands of dollars in cash flow, but a capital event can easily put millions of dollars on the scoreboard.

It's at this point in a project that you'll receive back the vast majority of your initial investment and profits. This is particularly exciting when it happens on account of a cash-out refinance. We'll discuss the cash-out refinance (and why it's such an amazing resource) in more depth later, but in short, it's a way for investors to realize any appreciation they've forced into the property's valuation through renovations and upgrades without actually having to sell the property.

Not all deals utilize a cash-out refinance, in which case the big payday comes upon selling the asset.

THE PREFERRED RETURN

Preferred returns are increasingly common these days. With the increasing popularity of syndications, a glut of operators have flooded the market. This provides an ample supply of deals for would-be passive investors to choose from.

Deal sponsors, in response, have searched for ways to make their offerings more compelling. The preferred return does just that. It's a powerful way to create alignment of interest between operators and their investors.

So what is this magical preferred return? Simply put, it's a minimum threshold return that limited partners must receive before the general partners receive their share of the equity split.

A deal offering a 7% preferred return means the limited partners will receive a minimum 7% return before the deal sponsors take their slice of the profit. If the deal underperforms (which often occurs in a deal's early years, during the renovation/reposition period), then there might not be enough cash flow to hit the 7% preferred return. In that instance, it's common for the preferred return to roll over into the next year.

Examples never hurt, so here we go. If we have a property that only returns 5% in year one, then in year two, the limited partners should receive 9% (to catch up and achieve an average return of 7% between the two years) before the general partners get anything.

Be aware, this isn't always the case. Some operators structure their deals so that unmet preferred returns simply disappear from year to year. A disappearing preferred return eliminates much of the reason for its existence in the first place, so get clear on this point before signing any paperwork.

Preferred returns are a way of putting the limited partner's interests before those of the sponsors. The general partners don't get paid unless the deal performs to a minimum standard. This really incentivizes them to achieve the projected returns.

Now, let's take a look at an equity split with preferred return factored in from the beginning. Our hypothetical deal offers a 70/30 split with 7% preferred return. Again, we've invested $100,000 out of a total $1,000,000 raise, giving us 10% of the units allocated to the limited partnership.

In year one, this deal only produces $50,000 of cash flow, of which your 10% share entitles you to $5,000. This year one return of 5% leaves you 2% short on your preferred return. Unfortunately, our general partners do not get to participate in this year's profits.

In year two, our operators have increased cash flow to $100,000. Of that, your preferred return entitles you to 9% (2% to make up for year one, and 7% for year two), or $9,000. You have now received $14,000 in total across the two years and your preferred return has been satisfied (for now).

But that's not all.

You'll notice that our year two cash-on-cash return was 10%. Of that, the limited partners only took 9%, leaving an extra 1% (or $1,000) yet to be distributed.

This $1,000 gets divided according to the equity split (70/30), with $700 going to the limited partners and $300 to the general partners. Your 10% of the limited partnership entitles you to an additional $70.

Huzzah! We're rich!

Okay, maybe not. Remember, this is simply an example to prove the concept. Unfortunately, not all deals are so straightforward. Things get really complicated really fast when we introduce hurdles, catch-ups, and dilutions.

CATCH-UP

Operators aren't doing these deals out of the goodness of their hearts. They're running a business and seeking a great return (just like you).

When a project first gets off the ground, it might fail to deliver a surplus of cash flow. Deal sponsors typically go a bit hungry during these early years to ensure their passive investors earn a strong return. Once the project stabilizes and the cash flow increases, general partners might seek to *catch up* to their passive investors.

If, throughout the project, the limited partners have earned a steady 7% preferred return while the general partners have only achieved a 2% return, the deal might be structured so that the sponsors are entitled to a disproportionate amount of any returns in surplus of the LP's 7% until the GP achieves a certain threshold (let's say, 5%).

Once the deal sponsors *catch up*, the equity split returns to its original orientation.

HURDLE

Hurdles are more common than catch-ups and a bit easier to understand. The hurdle shifts the equity split in favor of the deal sponsor as the project delivers certain benchmark results.

Here's how that might look. The equity split starts at 70/30 and remains there until the limited partners achieve a 15% return. Returns above and beyond 15% are split 50/50.

That's an example of a single hurdle, but you could easily imagine a scenario with multiple hurdles.

This structure works well to align the general partners' interests with their passive brethren. Deal sponsors are better rewarded for delivering higher returns. Limited partners enjoy this structure because while, yes, the split becomes less favorable to them, that only occurs because they've already achieved some great returns.

Hurdles create interesting win-win scenarios where the general partners are encouraged to take the long view on a project.

DILUTION / BUYOUT

This is our least favorite of the ways an equity split might shift in favor of the general partners. It's most common in a preferred equity or debt investment structure where the investor collects a set return throughout a deal's life cycle. These accruing returns dilute the passive investor's ownership in the entity.

Think of it as though the passive investor has been *paid back*, much like a bank mortgage. Once they receive their expected return, they're out of the deal, meaning they don't get to participate in the big equity upside at the sale of the project. If you're a risk-averse investor content with solid, consistent returns, then you might be very happy with this structure.

All told, there are countless ways to structure the equity split. Our preference is to err on the side of simplicity. In our opinion, unnecessarily complex waterfall structures should be avoided, but what constitutes "complex" varies by user.

Regardless of where you fall on the spectrum of mathematical sophistication, don't be afraid to ask questions or simply walk away from a deal if you don't understand the return structure. Many people fear asking a question that'll make them look stupid, and so they go with the flow despite not having a clue what's going on.

When it comes to investing in multifamily apartment syndications, there's no need to feel overwhelmed. Remember, it's better to do *no* deal than a *bad* deal. And a bad deal, in our book, is one you don't understand.

TAXES

"I am proud to be paying taxes in the United States. The only thing is, I could be just as proud for half of the money."

— Arthur Godfrey

When it comes to wealth creation, it's not about what you make, it's about what you keep.

To keep more of what you make, you have to reduce your expenses. For most people, the single greatest expense they incur each year is the one going to Uncle Sam.

Some of my closest friends are high-income-earning professionals (doctors, lawyers, architects, etc.) who make fantastic livings, but who end up paying back nearly 50% of what they earn in the form of taxes each year. When I speak to most of these friends about how they plan to mitigate their taxable liabilities, they look at me as though I've sprouted a second nose.

Most normal people don't spend much time thinking about taxes. They'll grumble once a year when it comes time to pay up, but it's usually such a convoluted and frustrating experience that they simply shut down and do the bare minimum when it comes time to file their taxes for the year.

As a result, they have no strategy for reducing their liabilities. Which is a shame, considering there are some simple and easily accessible ways to reduce taxable income available to everybody.

Owning real estate is one such strategy.

There's a reason the majority of wealthy people in the world own real estate and why they also, legally, pay very little in taxes proportional to what they earn. The average American simply doesn't realize they also have access to these vehicles.

Investments that utilize limited partnerships and LLCs open up a whole new world of tax-deferred possibilities thanks to the magic of depreciation and expense write-offs.

In many cases, with all of these factors at play, it's possible to reduce your tax exposure to zero (or even negative) despite benefiting from thousands of dollars of cash flow distributions each year.

Now, there are very few ways to completely eliminate tax liability (short of dying, and even then Uncle Sam will come knocking on your heir's door if you don't play your cards right). Reducing tax liability is mostly a game of kicking the can down the road. But if you play it right, you can kick that can pretty darn far.

Before we get too deep into the weeds, here's a quick disclaimer: We're not tax professionals, and this isn't tax advice. What follows is for informational purposes only. Consult with your tax professional before making any decisions that could impact your tax situation.

All right, let's hop into one of the most lucrative topics you'll ever study and learn about a few of the ways we can legally reduce taxable liability through owning real estate.

DEPRECIATION

When I first started investing in real estate, I focused mostly on all the "tangible" benefits sitting right in front of me, things like monthly cash flow, or the fact that I now owned a physical asset I could touch and feel.

It wasn't until we conducted a cost segregation study on that first apartment building that the light bulb went off in my head and I realized how incredible the tax benefits for owning real estate truly are.

To wrap your head around this, you have to first understand depreciation, which isn't the most intuitive of concepts. The IRS recognizes that nothing lasts forever and that everything wears out eventually. Everything comprising a building (carpet, paint, shingles, dishwashers, wiring, windows, etc.) loses value over time due to usage and age.

As a property wears out and *loses* value, the IRS allows those losses to be written off. These write-offs often completely offset the passive income earned through these assets. This means tax-deferred cash flow.

To calculate a property's depreciation schedule, we first deduct the value of the land the property sits on (land isn't depreciable). Generally this is 10–30% of the purchase price. To get a more specific number for your municipality, simply refer to the building's property tax information listed on the local property assessor's website.

For instance, if we purchase a building for $1,000,000 and allocate 20% to land value, then our building's value is $800,000. We divide this new building value ($800,000) by 27.5 (the number of years over which the IRS presumes our building will wear out), giving us $29,090 worth of passive losses each year.

Here's how that looks for you the passive investor.

You'll receive a K-1 each year for tax filing purposes. On it you will see how much you earned in passive income through the cash flow distributions produced by the property.

Let's say you invested $50,000 in the above property worth $1,000,000 (which, for the sake of simplicity, we'll assume was purchased without a bank loan). This gives you an ownership stake of 25%. In year one, you receive $5,000 worth of cash flow distributions (a solid 10% cash-on-cash return).

Your 25% ownership in the deal entitles you to 25% of the depreciation scheduled for the year. Of the $29,090 worth of total depreciation, you receive $7,272 (25%).

You'll see this number elsewhere on the K-1, signifying your passive losses for the year.

In a nutshell, although you only received $5,000 in cash flow distributions, you get to write off over $7,000 in losses.

This means you don't pay taxes on those distributions. Not yet, at least. Uncle Sam always gets his dues, and he'll come collecting for depreciation recapture when you sell the property. Don't worry, later in the chapter we'll discuss some strategies to avoid this.

Here's the important takeaway: thanks to the magic of depreciation, you likely won't pay any taxes on the cash flow distributions over the life of a project.

Pretty incredible, huh?

Now, in the immortal words of Billy Mays, but wait! There's more!

ACCELERATED DEPRECIATION, COST SEGREGATION STUDIES, AND BONUS DEPRECIATION

Things get even crazier when we enter the world of accelerated depreciation and cost segregation studies.

First, what the heck are accelerated depreciation and cost segregation studies? They're incredible tools, that's what.

See, it's ridiculous to assume that all the parts of a building wear out at the same rate, right?

Carpet ages differently than windows, which wear out on a different timetable than the plumbing.

Some of these things might last twenty-seven-and-a-half years, others only fifteen. Others might only have a good five or seven years in them. The IRS recognizes this and allows us to write off all the myriad parts of a building according to an accelerated depreciation schedule unique to each item.

If this sounds difficult and time-consuming, that's because it is. Most operators that don't want to risk making a mistake hire this job out to a third-party engineering firm that'll provide a detailed depreciation schedule unique to *your* property.

The craziest part of all (though it might not still exist by the time you read this) is bonus depreciation, which allows us to claim the entire depreciation schedule in year one.

No spreading it out, just taking it all in one lump sum from the beginning. And since passive losses carry through from year to year, there's nothing to lose.

Remember, depreciation is a game of kick the can. Eventually you run out of road and Uncle Sam's gonna come looking for his cut when you sell the property. That is, unless you have some unique deferral strategies in your back pocket, strategies such as the 1031 exchange or Delaware Statutory Trust.

1031 EXCHANGE

Meet the golden goose of real estate investing. When successfully implemented, the 1031 exchange allows investors to sell one property and roll all the proceeds into a new property without paying any capital gains tax. It's an incredible strategy, but not without some drawbacks.

First, the strict timing guidelines make executing a 1031 a little like threading a needle while riding a motorcycle down a dirt road. These things are not terribly easy to execute.

Second, this might be a moot point for passive investors in an apartment syndication. One of the caveats of a 1031 exchange is that it must be for a "like-kind" exchange—namely, real estate for real estate. Unfortunately, as you may recall from our earlier conversations about syndication structures, you don't actually own the real estate in a private placement. You own a percentage of the company that owns the real estate, and that's an important distinction. There are ways around this involving Tenant in Common (TIC) structures, but they can get pricey and most operators won't entertain that option if you're bringing less than $1,000,000 to the table.

If you currently own some properties and want to cash out and go entirely passive, then your best bet might be to consider the Delaware Statutory Trust.

DELAWARE STATUTORY TRUST

Operators looking to create a Delaware Statutory Trust (DST) have to jump through a lot of hoops. These hoops, plus some potential limitations of this vehicle, mean very few players in the game actually create DSTs.

Generally, DSTs are the purview of large, institutional-grade investments that offer marginal, yet incredibly stable, returns.

All the reasons for this lie beyond the scope of this book. For now, just realize that if you've built up a decent portfolio and want to ride off into the sunset and live off a steady stream of cash flow, then the DST might be perfect for you.

CAPITAL GAINS TAX

If neither the 1031 exchange or DST sound viable, then unfortunately at some point you'll have to bite the depreciation recapture bullet and pay the capital gains tax.

Capital gains tax is between 15 and 25% (depending on your income), whereas depreciation recapture is taxed at your normal income tax rate.

It's nice to optimize the time value of your money by holding on to more of it (to be reinvested, for instance) through the magic of depreciation, so some investors go one step further and simply execute a buy-and-hold-forever strategy.

Without a sale, there's no capital gains tax or depreciation recapture. Problem solved, right? Probably not. Syndications typically consist of other investors eager to reclaim their capital sooner than never. Getting them all to agree to hold the property indefinitely is a tough sell.

It's also worth taking into consideration the velocity of capital when calculating whether it's better to sell early and take the tax hit or hold indefinitely.

From the numbers we've seen, the most efficient use of capital is to cash out when the IRR peaks in around years five through seven, pay the taxes, and reinvest. But again, run those numbers for yourself.

This isn't a book on taxes, so we're not even going to attempt to dive in to the full breadth of potential benefits and implications here. There are myriad strategies and loopholes and potential pitfalls to be cognizant of. If you want to brush up on all these strategies, we highly recommend you pick a book specifically on the topic. The potential savings you could realize across the span of your investments are enormous.

PART THREE

THE BUSINESS MODEL

CHAPTER 8

REAL ESTATE 101: ASSET CLASS

"Our brains are either our greatest assets
or our greatest liabilities."

— Robert Kiyosaki

There are countless ways to make money in real estate. Thus far we've primarily touched on apartment syndications, and I've alluded to my foray into the small residential game with my first triplex.

Even if you're intending to focus on multifamily, it's important you have a broad view of the playing field to understand the different property types, property classes, and business models frequently employed in the pursuit of incredible returns.

We have a particular niche (Class B/C value-add multifamily). By the end of this chapter, you'll understand exactly what all that means and have a good sense for the alternatives.

ASSET CLASSES

It's not uncommon to hear people talk about the different asset classes within real estate, but that's technically not correct (though the difference is one of simple semantics). There are five asset classes, and they are grouped based on common characteristics that behave similarly in the marketplace.

Within these five, three are considered traditional:

1. Equities (stocks)
2. Fixed income (bonds)
3. Cash equivalents (money markets)

And two are considered alternative (though still extremely common):

4. Real estate
5. Commodities

There's never any shortage of disagreement in the world, and I'm sure plenty of people out there would add other asset classes to the list (like cryptocurrency or collectibles), but let's not split hairs. What's important for our purposes here is that real estate is the *asset class*. Beneath that, we can further subdivide into property type and property class. From there, we then establish our business plan (or strategy).

Let's dive in from the top and break the real estate asset class into its four primary property types:

- Residential
- Industrial
- Land
- Commercial Real Estate (CRE)

Generally, when people talk about multifamily commercial real estate, they're talking about properties with five or more units. Assets with fewer than five units are considered *residential* (similar to condos and single-family homes), as this is the type of loan utilized in acquiring these properties.

Before we tackle commercial real estate, let's first address industrial and land.

"Industrial" can refer to a whole lot of things, including manufacturing, distribution centers, and warehouses. Few sectors have grown more than the industrial sector in recent years. Online retailers have increasingly moved toward large distribution centers located in close proximity to large metropolitan areas, creating solid demand for this type of commercial real estate.

While industrial is hot and on the rise, then land is the tried-and-true, never going out of style option. Land, on a long enough time frame, tends to always find itself on the winning side of the supply and demand curve.

Why?

Because unless Elon Musk succeeds in getting us to Mars, there's a finite amount of ground to go around.

While land is generally desirable, it's also risky because it doesn't generate cash flow, takes years to generate any sort of return, and carries with it a certain element of *speculation*. With land, as with other speculative opportunities, you either win big or lose big.

Which brings us to the mack daddy of real estate property types (or at least, the mack daddy for the purposes of this book): commercial real estate. The broad category of commercial real estate includes multifamily, retail, office, self-storage, mobile home parks, and more.

Each category has its unique strengths and weaknesses. Here's a high-level overview of the most popular commercial real estate sub-types.

COMMERCIAL REAL ESTATE SUB-ASSET TYPES

Multifamily

At five units and above, you're squarely in the realm of commercial multi-family. Multifamily is the golden child of investing because of its perceived safety coupled with high returns. Even at the height of the financial crisis, the delinquency rate never spiked above 1%.

Retail / Office

Retail includes brick-and-mortar shopping experiences like malls, strip centers, and single-tenant buildings (like a Burger King). Office is similar in that it can have single or multiple-tenant properties.

Retail has taken a beating in recent years with e-commerce giants taking a significant slice out of their bottom line. Even so, there are still great opportunities to be found. Be aware that building valuations get fairly complicated once lease terms and anchor tenant strength get factored in.

Office, likewise, has struggled greatly with the recent cultural shift to remote working.

One of the great things about retail and office is that tenants tend to stay much longer (sometimes signing leases up to thirty years). When paired with triple net leases (NNN) (meaning the tenant pays for upgrades, repairs, taxes, etc.) you have the perfect storm for solid, consistent returns while having to do practically zero work.

Self-Storage

Self-storage is one of the fastest growing (and most stable) of all commercial real estate investments. Incredible demand coupled with limited operator overhead makes these assets easy to operate and quite profitable. No tenants, toilets, or trash. What's not to love?

These assets produce great cash flow but not terribly impressive appreciation. That's what you get when it's relatively easy and cost-effective for the competition to simply build a new structure across the street.

Self-storage is the darling of recession-resistant investment opportunities. The theory is that, as the market softens and people lose their jobs, they will opt to downsize their living arrangements in the short term, thus needing a place to store their possessions until things rebound.

On the other hand, when times are good and people buy more and more things, it's only logical that they should need a place to store them all.

Either way, self-storage wins.

Mobile Home Parks

Another recession-resistant property type with a capped supply is mobile home parks.

With most mobile home parks developed in the '70s and earlier, and a complete lack of new inventory being built, there's a lot of aging infrastructure, aging owners, and capped supply. This creates unique opportunities for savvy investors. As a result, mobile home parks have increased in popularity with investors in recent years.

There are many more sub-types of commercial real estate. We could spend thousands of pages picking apart the nuances of each and every one. The concepts you'll learn throughout this book will serve you regardless of which property type you pursue.

For the purposes of this book, moving forward, we'll focus exclusively on multifamily apartment buildings.

Now that we know our asset classes, property types, and sub-property types, it's time to peel back another layer to talk about property class.

PROPERTY CLASS

Commercial real estate is graded based on age and quality. This scale utilizes letters (like a report card) ranging from A to D.

Let's break down these classes to understand how they might fit into your investing profile.

Class A

Class A properties are premium apartments located in the most desirable neighborhoods within the best school districts. The interiors are new and modern, typically utilizing hardwood floors, granite countertops, and stainless-steel appliances.

Additionally, these properties typically include top-shelf amenities including on-site gyms, covered garage parking, patios, pools, and dog parks. Generally, Class A buildings were built within the past ten years and command top-dollar rents.

Brand-new buildings have zero deferred maintenance, meaning very little opportunity to deploy the value-add model on these assets. Class A properties tend to attract institutional and risk-averse investors seeking decent cash flow, a hedge against inflation, and tax benefits with limited downside.

Class B

One step down are Class B properties built within the past twenty to forty years (although age is a moving target depending on who you talk to).

These properties are located in nice neighborhoods within proximity of desirable amenities such as Target, Starbucks, or Whole Foods. The scope of amenities is similar to that of Class A properties, just a bit more dated. With little to no deferred maintenance, Class B apartments rent out at the upper end of the market, but less so than their newer Class A counterparts.

These assets present an opportunity to execute the value-add model as they age. When implemented properly, these deals can return great dividends with limited downsides.

Class C

Class C properties are generally buildings constructed between thirty and fifty years ago. Again, age isn't the most important variable. It's possible to completely renovate an old building up to Class A or B standard. Class C properties may not sparkle, but they're also not falling over.

These buildings often have a healthy amount of deferred maintenance. Most systems (roofs, paint, flooring, appliances) have reached or are nearing the end of their useful life. Inside these units, kitchens and bathrooms are dated, often sporting linoleum flooring or carpet, plus "vintage" appliances.

These properties are prime value-add opportunities. Improving the interiors and exteriors often justifies increasing rents a notch below their Class B counterparts.

Class C properties are the bread-and-butter of our value-add model. We love these buildings because they usually have deferred maintenance, dated furnishings, and (more often than not) burnt out mom-and-pop owners. All of this creates a perfect storm of opportunity.

Class D

Tread lightly, my friend.

Class D properties are run-down buildings with incredible amounts of deferred maintenance, located in the types of neighborhoods you don't want to walk around after dark.

With heaps worth of structural and mechanical issues, these neglected buildings are on their last legs.

If you're considering a Class D property, best make certain the deal sponsor has experience operating this type of asset, or you might get more than you bargained for. Class D properties are not for the faint of heart. They pose significant operational issues, both from a maintenance and repair perspective, and often come with a problematic tenant base that can make rental collections incredibly difficult.

Of course, there are potential upsides to be had with these assets. Then again, they can also prove to be a literal worst nightmare.

Don't say you weren't warned.

CHAPTER 9

REAL ESTATE 201: STRATEGY

"Hope is not a strategy."

— Vince Lombardi

I've been a competitive chess player since I was a little kid. Growing up, I read every chess book and magazine I could get my hands on.

In one particular magazine, I found an interview with the former World Champion Anatoly Karpov, who is widely considered the greatest chess strategist of all time. His archrival—and eventual heir to his throne— Garry Kasparov (a name you might recognize from his epic battle against the computer Deep Blue), on the other hand, is considered the greatest tactician of all time.

What's the difference between a *strategy* and a *tactic*? In that interview, Karpov explained it like this: **"Strategy is knowing what to do when there is nothing to do. Tactics are knowing what to do when there** *is* something to do."

That's a good definition, but if you haven't spent much of your life pontificating on the differences between strategy and tactics, then a simpler definition might serve our purposes better.

Strategy is *what* you do. Tactics are *how* you do it.

There are countless strategies real estate investors employ to make money. Here are three of the most common.

THREE COMMON STRATEGIES

Buy-and-Hold

The buy-and-hold strategy means purchasing a property with the intention of holding it indefinitely. Often these properties are passed down from generation to generation, making them fantastic legacy builders.

Buy-and-hold is a tried-and-true strategy that, on a long enough time-horizon, always delivers exceptional results. And because you don't have the intention of selling, short-term fluctuations in property value don't matter.

Some investors set the goal of paying off all the debt on these properties so that, within thirty years, they own these things outright. Short of Armageddon, it's hard to lose money on a completely paid-off property. And yet this isn't usually the highest and best use of capital. With this strategy, you could theoretically have hundreds of thousands (if not millions) of dollars' worth of equity tied up in a property.

That's effectively dead money.

A more efficient use of that equity could be realized by employing occasional cash-out refinances, home equity lines of credit, or home equity loans to redeploy that capital into other investments.

It's hard to go wrong with the buy-and-hold strategy, though it should be noted that nobody gets rich quickly with a long-term hold. When people say real estate is the best way to get rich slowly but surely, they're usually talking about the buy-and-hold strategy.

Fix-and-Flip

The fix-and-flip strategy looks to force appreciation into an asset and then extract that value as quickly as possible. This strategy maximizes the velocity of capital by getting in, boosting returns, and getting out before the time value of money starts weakening the newly created equity.

Pulling capital out of a fix-and-flip could occur by selling the asset or by refinancing the property with the intention of transitioning into a buy-and-hold.

Many new investors get their start in real estate through the fix-and-flip strategy. It's not unreasonable to double or triple your start-up capital in a surprisingly short time frame, but it does require a combination of good timing, solid underwriting, and operational experience.

For most people, fix-and-flip calls to mind the television shows where some spunky real estate investor buys a shanty for $10, fixes it up with some fancy backsplashes, and then sells it for $300,000 five months later. That's one way of executing the fix-and-flip strategy.

Equally viable (and our favorite) is to boost the net operating income (NOI) of an apartment building by increasing rents and decreasing expenses through the value-add tactic.

Development

Drive through any thriving major metropolitan area and you'll see all sorts of new buildings being erected, ranging from single-family homes all the way up to skyscrapers. These are all forms of development.

This strategy can produce incredible returns because you've created something of immense value where once there was nothing. Unfortunately, the act of creation is fraught with risk. Building a skyscraper or a single-family home is no exception. If you've ever hired a contractor to do any sort of project on your home, you're aware of how often those projects run over time and budget.

Development deals have a fair number of potential pitfalls, which creates a high barrier to successful entry in terms of operator expertise and proficiency. Despite the potential difficulties, this sector can be incredibly lucrative. Either way, if you're going to play in this sandbox, you'd best know exactly what you're doing.

FOUR COMMON TACTICS

Now that we know a couple of the most popular commercial real estate investing strategies, let's dive in to *how* to employ these strategies.

Core

In the stock market, core investments are a portfolio's safe-and-secure foundational holdings. They're the mainstay of risk-averse (i.e. conservative) investors looking for stable income with low risk.

Real estate core assets are the highest quality properties located in close proximity to an urban hub. These are the fancy new buildings going up all over town.

We call these trophy properties. They look great and you'll feel some pride in owning them. These assets, on the downside, don't generate stupendous returns (often between 3 and 7% annualized).

For a certain type of investor (the type who invest in REITs, for example), core assets are perfect. They require little in the way of asset management, are typically occupied by credit-worthy tenants, and utilize low leverage.

Leverage is an important aspect to consider. A brand-new building leveraged to the hilt (90% LTV, for instance) increases the risk profile and no longer qualifies as a core investment.

Overall, core assets offer the best opportunity for capital preservation on long holds in a low-risk environment.

Core-Plus

Investors seeking core-plus opportunities are still mighty risk-averse, though they're generally seeking both growth and income (with a bent toward income).

These are high-quality assets that maintain solid occupancy. Still, there's usually opportunity to improve these properties through light renovations and operational efficiencies.

These buildings, compared to core, require more active management and are starting to carry some deferred maintenance. A little goes a long way, however, and often it's enough to simply improve the curb appeal and make light cosmetic improvements to the interiors of these properties.

You'll often find more meat on these returns (between 8 and 10% annually) than you would in a core asset.

Again, debt plays a large part in the risk profile of these assets and operators will often maintain low (50–60%) leverage.

Value-Add

Welcome to the most popular tactic amongst syndicators (ourselves included). Because this tactic is so popular, we'll dive deep into the value-add model later in this chapter, complete with a case study to help you wrap your head around this amazing business model.

From a high level, this model revolves around operators increasing a building's value by forcing appreciation. When properly executed, the returns on value-add opportunities are quite impressive (15–20% annually), while still maintaining a solid hedge against risk by utilizing relatively conservative amounts of leverage (60–80%).

The value-add strategy relies heavily upon an operator's ability to accurately forecast and execute a business plan. Core and core-plus assets, by comparison, are most easily put on autopilot. Value-add investors don't have that luxury. They must remain vigilant and on top of their game at all times.

Opportunistic

What's that you say? "Risk" is just a four-letter word? All right adrenaline junkie, this might be the business model for you.

Opportunistic deals carry the most risk of all the tactics we've discussed. These projects tend to be complex multifaceted beasts that don't produce any sort of return for the first couple of years.

Opportunistic is like *value-add* on steroids (or crack).

These projects include ground-up development, repurposing entire buildings, or simply purchasing completely vacant buildings. While value-add projects are often nearly stabilized and generating enough cash flow to support the asset's ongoing existence, opportunistic deals exist on the other end of the spectrum, operating on the razor's edge of viability.

The ultimate success or failure of an opportunistic project relies heavily on the operator's expertise and ability to accurately execute the business plan.

Opportunistic investors typically utilize the maximum leverage they can get their hands on. The result of these projects' massive potential upside is annual returns easily exceeding 20%.

BRINGING IT ALL TOGETHER

The pieces of the strategy and tactics puzzle can go together in countless ways.

One project might be a core-plus buy-and-hold focused on solid returns baked into a stable asset. Another project might be a fix-and-flip value-add coupling big appreciation with solid cash flow. Then again, if you live on the wild side, you might pursue some opportunistic redevelopment of a Class D property in a soon-to-be Class B neighborhood.

We love the value-add business model because it allows us to improve our buildings' value while also maintaining solid cash flow. Most apartment syndications you'll encounter revolve around the value-add business model. So, with that in mind, we'll spend the rest of this chapter on the specifics of this tactic.

CHAPTER 10

REAL ESTATE MASTER CLASS: VALUE-ADD

"All intelligent investing is value investing—
acquiring more than you are paying for."

— Charlie Munger

The biggest complaint I had with my first property (that triplex) was that I had zero control over its value. External market forces dictated its value regardless of how well I operated the property.

If the market goes up, we call that **organic appreciation**. If the market goes down, we call that a **bummer**.

If you own your home and have seen its value increase, then you're familiar with this concept. That's organic appreciation.

While it's important to calculate organic appreciation into your underwriting assumptions, your model shouldn't rely on this mostly uncontrollable factor. Markets currently experiencing strong economic and population growth will see higher appreciation than markets with weak economies and fleeing populations (Austin versus Detroit, for example).

Those same factors tend to play out on the neighborhood level as well. For instance, in St. Paul, Minnesota (where we primarily invest), one neighborhood has seen appreciation close to 10% in the past twelve months, whereas the neighborhood directly bordering it to the east only saw half that growth, at around 5%.

Many factors account for these differences. Here's the important takeaway: *don't bank on organic appreciation.*

If your deal sponsor projects an asset will appreciate a certain percentage year over year without justifying that growth through the use of historical trends, knowledge of future development, or some other large macro-economic event, then consider these projections hyper-critically.

We recommend running a sensitivity analysis to see if the numbers still work without the optimistic appreciation assumptions. The numbers you want to challenge most critically revolve around revenue growth, expense growth, and exit capitalization rate (aka the cap rate, which we'll explain in-depth shortly). Here's how to do that.

FORCED APPRECIATION

Forced appreciation is the opposite of organic appreciation and serves as the backbone of the value-add model. In the world of large multifamily, three levers dictate a property's value: revenue, expenses, and cap rate. Of these three levers, we control two of them.

These three levers are important because commercial real estate is valued like a business. We can improve our property's value by operating it well.

Or, put differently, we're in control.

It's critical that we increase our building's value in this model, but how do we actually do that? It's one thing to say, "Add value." It's another thing entirely to put boots on the ground and actually execute the business plan. Let's break down the value-add model and discuss these three levers in more detail.

REVENUE

Rent

The most obvious way to grow revenue is by increasing the rent, but it's hard to justify charging more for a thing without somehow improving it. Eventually, the tenants will leave, and if the units are old, outdated, and not up to market standard, your operator will struggle to find new tenants.

The key is to find assets collecting below-market rents and then improve the facilities enough to justify raising rents in line with comparable buildings in the area. Properties requiring cosmetic improvements to the units and amenities are best. Common upgrades that lead to a significant increase in rent include new flooring, cabinets, countertops, appliances, paint, and amenities.

Improvements should justify a rent premium. Don't waste money over-improving units with materials and finishes excessive for the area and property class.

If we increase rents by even $100 per unit, then the downstream impact on our building's value can be worth millions of dollars. Extrapolating that out, $100 per month equals $1,200 a year. If the apartment complex has one hundred units, then that's an additional $120,000 in rental income per year. That's a fantastic improvement to the annual cash flow, no doubt, but that's not even the best part.

Remember, to calculate a commercial property's value we divide net operating income by cap rate (Value = NOI/Cap Rate).

If the market cap rate is 7%, then the asset's value has increased by over $1.7 million ($120,000/7% = $1,714,285). That's $1,714,285 worth of forced appreciation, just by increasing rents by $100 per unit.

Are you starting to see why we love the value-add model?

Things get wild when we successfully execute a cash-out refinance to realize that hidden equity. Often we're returning up to 60% of our investor's initial capital in a tax-free event. If you take that money and reinvest, well, now you're earning double returns on the same money. That's what we call maximizing the velocity of your capital.

KEY CONCEPT

Velocity of Capital
The velocity of capital is the frequency at which one unit of currency is used to purchase goods and services within a given time period. The more times we can use that single dollar within a window of time, the higher our velocity of capital.

Banks are great at maximizing the velocity of their capital. They'll take a single dollar that you've deposited in a savings account and borrow it out multiple times over (often to multiple borrowers simultaneously) in the form of loans. Because they're only required to maintain a portion of that lent capital in physical reserves, they're able to effectively clone a single dollar and make it work multiple full-time jobs simultaneously.

Most people don't realize they can do the same thing. We'll discuss the cash-out refinance in more detail shortly and show how exactly that works.

Supplemental Income

Raising rents is the tried-and-true method for increasing our top-line revenue, but it's not the only method available. Savvy operators recognize that small increases to other revenue streams can have profound effects. What might not seem like a consequential increase to residents can pay massive dividends to investors.

Here are some popular ways of increasing supplemental revenue.

Parking

Depending on an asset's location, parking might be considered a highly sought-after item. Densely packed urban centers typically struggle to offer sufficient parking. Residents in these areas happily pay a small monthly fee to avoid parking on the street.

Laundry

Coin-operated laundry is a staple of Class B and C multifamily assets. Class A properties often have in-unit machines (a convenience that usually justifies a rent premium). Many operators outsource the leasing of their laundry machines to third-party services who handle maintenance, repairs, and collections. In exchange, the operators take a small cut of the collected monthly revenue. It's our preference to handle these tasks in-house because it means more revenue hits our bottom line, which ultimately lands back in our investors' pockets).

Storage

Self-storage is usually in high demand. Humans tend to collect stuff over the years. Offering a convenient on-site solution for resident storage is an easy way to bring in extra revenue with very little work.

Pet Fees

Animal lovers know how difficult it is to find a decent place to rent that allows pets. Many operators don't allow pets, fearing it leads to more wear-and-tear on the units and potentially more issues with noise complaints and safety issues. On the whole, we find pets to be a net positive to our apartment communities. With this in mind, we happily accept pets for a fee.

EXPENSES

We divide expenses into two broad categories (excluding debt): utility and operations.

Utilities

Utility expenses stem from an inefficient building. It could have leaky pipes, an inefficient boiler, or poorly sealed windows letting all the heat out (or in!). There are two ways to decrease utilities.

1. Fix the problem so the building runs efficiently.
2. Pass responsibility for individual utilities (water and electricity in particular) to the tenants.

That first fix can get quite expensive and falls under the category of capital expenditures. CapEx improvements differ from repairs and maintenance in that they improve the life and longevity of the building.

Certain CapEx items are easier to deal with than others. Issues with underground plumbing, the foundation, and pretty much any electrical issue we've ever seen are some areas that almost always cause a big headache.

Once the major issues causing a building to bleed money every month have been addressed, savvy operators implement a program called Ratio Utility Billback Systems (RUBS). RUBS allows operators to bill residents for their utility usage (namely water and electricity). This simple program can decrease the utility bill by up to 80%. It's an incredibly powerful way to decrease expenses, to say the least.

Operational Expenses

Utilities are technically considered an operational expense, but for our purposes here we're splitting these up even further.

Your greatest business expense is walking around on two legs.

If you've ever operated a business, you'll understand the truth in that piece of wisdom.

Successfully operating an apartment community means having a number of boots on the ground. There's the maintenance team, the leasing agents, the property manager, and the lawyers, to name just a few.

Operational inefficiencies proliferate as more people become involved. Communication, oversight, and accountability naturally become increasingly murky with each new body added to the equation.

Fantastic operators understand how to cultivate a culture of excellence so that everybody on the team plays up to their highest potential. When this occurs, expenses drop, quality of work improves, and customer satisfaction goes through the roof.

It's a win-win-win.

With that said, these types of improvements are some of the most difficult to implement. Many new operators step into the game thinking cutting expenses will be a cinch, only to later discover they were woefully mistaken.

When somebody starts talking about how they're going to add value by decreasing operational expenses, I tend to get a little skeptical unless they have a track record of having done just that.

Nonetheless, if you find an operator skilled at this singular aspect of value-add, cling to them like a life raft. They're worth their weight in gold.

CAPITALIZATION RATE (CAP RATE)

Welcome to the most misunderstood term in all of real estate investing. If you're seeing the words "capitalization rate" for the first time, then you have no idea what we're talking about anyway. Let's strip it down to the basics.

First, a working definition.

Capitalization Rate (Cap Rate): The rate of return the market expects from a particular real estate investment in a particular area.

Was that helpful? No, probably not.

Let's simplify even more.

The cap rate signals how much the market values an asset at a particular moment in time.

Here's the theory: if we purchase an asset at a 7% cap rate with all cash, then we would receive a 7% cash-on-cash return.

In reality it doesn't work like that because closing fees, cap ex budget, and reserves aren't often considered in the calculation. This makes the cap rate a fairly hypothetical number.

So where does this magical number come from and what's it *actually* good for?

First, because the cap rate indicates market sentiment, we have to keep in mind that it's not static. It's constantly moving, though quite slowly. We calculate the current cap rate by looking at recent transactions of a similar asset type in a particular market. That is, what have others recently paid for comparable assets?

Yes, we're back to that *comparables* approach to property valuation that we railed so hard against in small residential properties. The difference here is that the cap rate only accounts for one-third of the levers we can pull when it comes to increasing our asset's value. It's not perfect, but it's better than the alternative.

Here's the frustrating thing you might have noticed about cap rates: because cap rates are based on comparable recent transactions, there's a fair bit of subjectivity involved when calculating. It's like comparing apples to oranges while using a banana as the standard.

Usually we opt out of playing such games. Unfortunately, when it comes to commercial real estate and cap rates, you don't have that luxury.

Earlier we asked, what's the cap rate good for? It's this: the cap rate is a multiplier used in calculating a building's value. The tricky bit is that the cap rate is *inversely correlated* to a property's value. The higher the cap rate, the lower the building's valuation.

A tad confusing, yeah?

I don't usually turn to math when I need things simplified, but in this case it'll prove helpful.

Let's assume we have access to a parallel universe. In one world we purchase a building at a 10% cap rate, and in the other world, we purchase that same building at a 5 cap.

If both buildings have an NOI of $100,000 and we apply the magic formula to calculate a building's value (NOI / Cap Rate = Value), we find that our buildings are worth the following:

$100,000 / **10%** = $1,000,000

$100,000 / **5%** = $2,000,000

Sellers seek lower cap rates whereas buyers hunt for higher cap rates.

Many new investors make the unnecessary mistake of setting a benchmark cap rate and refusing to purchase anything below that number. These investors say things like, "I only buy at 10 cap." Talk about an overly simplistic way of utilizing cap rates.

Passive investors don't need to understand all the nuances of the cap rate. To apply the knowledge you've now gathered, we have to resolve a quasi-paradoxical issue.

First, cap rates are inherently squishy and subjective.

Second, cap rates are the single most important number in determining a building's value.

So what do we do? How do we treat this all-important number?

Step one: ignore the cap rate at acquisition. This might seem counterintuitive, but cap rates are largely irrelevant when purchasing a property. We underwrite to deliver certain return benchmarks. If our underwriting suggests we can hit those returns, then we move forward with the project, regardless of the cap rate at acquisition.

Step two: assume the exit cap rate will be *worse* than the acquisition cap rate. Nobody can predict the future. Everybody's crystal ball is equally murky.

To overcome this lack of prescience, just assume the world will be worse in the future than it is at present. If during underwriting we assume a worse exit cap rate than when we purchased, then we'll be pleasantly surprised should reality prove less horrible than anticipated. More importantly, we won't be caught swimming without our bathing suit should our doom-and-gloom prediction of the future prove accurate.

Passive investors should look for this in a deal sponsor's underwriting. If it's not immediately obvious, simply ask, "What's acquisition cap rate versus projected exit cap rate?"

If the exit cap rate is lower than at acquisition, you have, in our opinion, a dangerously optimistic operator on your hand. Tread lightly.

Value-Add Case Study

The first time somebody explained a value-add apartment syndication to me, it sounded like pure voodoo-math-magic.

It took walking through a couple of examples before it clicked and I finally understood enough to believe in the model. Though, honestly, even after having executed this business plan multiple times over and having realized millions of dollars' worth of gains, it still doesn't feel quite real.

With that in mind, let's run through an example to help you wrap your mind around the interplay between all the different variables. Understanding the different value-add levers will help you not only distinguish between good and bad deals, but also good and bad operators.

We designed the infographic below to educate and illustrate a point. It's simple by design. In its simplicity there are a few great learning opportunities of what things you need to be on the lookout for when diving into an apartment syndication.

Once you fully digest this example, you'll have a better understanding of how the value-add model works, plus you'll be well-armed against shiny opportunities with questionable assumptions.

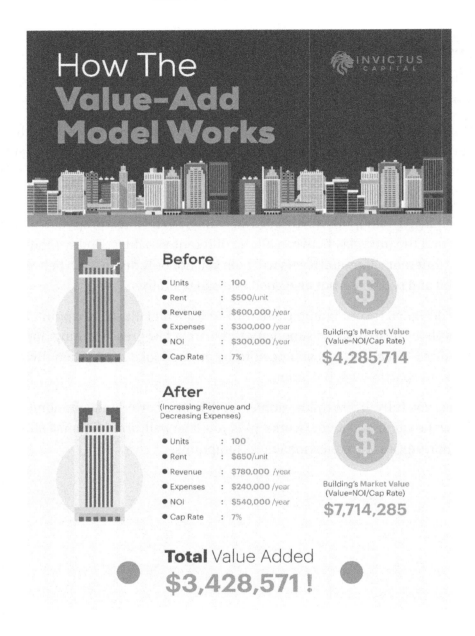

The entire value-add model hinges upon this formula: **Building Value = Net Operating Income / Cap Rate**

Remember, we calculate NOI by subtracting operational expenses (not including debt service) from gross revenue.

We don't include debt because we don't want the lending term, which is always different depending on the operator, to dictate the value of our building. Instead, we ignore the debt for now and simply look at the net profit of the basic business. As we do so, we realize there are two ways to increase the value of our building: **increase revenue and decrease expenses**.

INCREASING REVENUE

Let's first examine the revenue growth assumptions. Average monthly rent before acquisition is $500 per unit. Upon completing the renovations, we're able to get a $50 rent premium, increasing monthly rent to $550.

Here's the first question: **Is this reasonable?**

The answer to that question depends on the local market, but generally we look for opportunities to raise rents by $150–200 per unit. Deals with more upside typically require a lot more renovation. Under $100 worth of rent premium could signify a thin deal. For now, let's assume this is an achievable assumption.

If we answer the first question affirmatively, then the second question is: **How do we realize these gains?**

These revenue gains will come either through rental or supplemental income growth. Making unit-level improvements that justify higher rents is the tried-and-true best method to boost revenue. Cosmetic improvements in the form of new flooring, cabinets, appliances, fixtures, and paint are amongst the most common upgrades that can fetch a rent premium on a modest budget.

Supplemental income shouldn't be overlooked, however. Massive value can be added to a property through parking, pet, and storage fees, not to mention coin-operated laundry or bundled internet packages.

The next part of the equation to consider is expenses.

DECREASING EXPENSES

Here's one of the most valuable business lessons I've ever learned: *a dollar saved is worth more than a dollar earned.*

It's a simple concept that carries so much weight.

If we're operating a business on a 50% margin, then for every one dollar of increased revenue, we get to keep fifty cents. On the other hand, if we cut out a dollar worth of expenses, then that's pure in-our-pocket profit. In this example, saving a dollar is twice as valuable as earning one.

There's a certain sexiness to increasing revenue. In sports, we idolize the guys and gals scoring the points, not the ones stopping the other team from scoring. We tend to remember the names of the All-Time High-Scorer, not the All-Time High-Blocker.

But remember, defense wins championships, even if the defense tends to be the unsung heroes.

If you want to be a successful real estate investor, keep the following maxim at the forefront of your mind: *it's not how much you make, it's how much you keep.*

Now that we're on the same wavelength about the importance of cutting expenses, let's dive in to the expense column of the infographic above.

Before acquisition, expenses are $300,000, which represents 50% of the total revenue. This expense ratio is an important number when evaluating an operator's underwriting.

A 50% operational expense budget represents a conservative base-line assumption when underwriting apartment complexes. A well-run operation with in-house management will have an expense ratio closer to 35–40%. Much lower than this and the underwriting becomes suspect. They're either cutting corners or, worse, they don't realize they're cutting corners.

All right, dear reader, if ever there were a time to pay attention, it's now. Here's a great learning moment.

Notice how, after acquisition, the expenses decreased to $240,000. Assuming the revenue stays the same (at $600,000), then our expense ratio of 40% is exactly what we would expect from a well-run asset.

This, however, is an example of how easily we can be misled if we don't understand how the whole system fits together.

The astute observer will notice the error: The after-acquisition example doesn't account for the *increased* revenue (remember, we boosted that from $600,000 to $780,000). Once we divide our *new* revenue by expenses, we find our expense ratio is actually 30%!

How much does this change the end valuation of the building?

Well, if we plug in a more conservative expense ratio of 40%, then our total expenses are $312,000, which drops our net operating income down to $468,000 ($780,000 − $312,000). To calculate our building's new valuation, we divide NOI by cap rate ($468,000 / 7%) to discover our building is now only worth $6,685,714.

Just like that, our building lost over a million dollars in projected value on account of a small oversight. It's still a great deal, but it raises some questions.

Is this a case of malicious underwriting designed to mislead investors or an honest mistake?

To answer that question, we turn to the operator. How they respond tells you a lot of about them as a potential partner.

If they answer by explaining they're a vertically integrated full-service firm with their own in-house construction crew operating a handful of similar properties in the immediate surrounding area of this prospective acquisition and their historical expenses on those properties hover around 30% (and they can provide some evidence of that claim), then you might have a rock-star operator on your hands. With that said, an expense ratio below 35% still stretches belief.

If they give any other answer, including, "Oh, that was an oversight," then tread carefully. They're either new, stupid, or unscrupulous. Don't do business with people who check any two of those three boxes.

NUMBERS CAN BE MADE TO LIE

It's a recurring theme, but it can't be overstated: *the passive investor's most important job is to vet the general partner.*

Deals can be easily manipulated in any number of ways to show whatever type of projection an operator wants to see. We'll show you some of the numbers that often get tweaked to deliver overly enthusiastic returns, but your best protection comes from working with top-notch operators that you *know, like, trust,* and who have a track record of excellence.

We'll talk about some ways to put a deal sponsor through the ringer, but first, a bonus round.

There's one last assumption in the infographic above that needs to be considered with a critical eye. It doesn't necessarily point to nefarious underwriting practices, but it does suggest the operator hasn't been sufficiently conservative in their projections.

Can you find it?

I'll give you a hint: *it has something to do with the exit cap rate.*

PART FOUR

THE PASSIVE INVESTOR'S JOB

CHAPTER 11
VETTING OPERATORS

"Bet on the jockey, not the horse."

- Proverb

I play a pick-up game of tennis with my buddy every week. We are "enthusiastically remedial." We're not great, but at the end of the day, we have fun.

Now, given what little you know of my tennis prowess, how do you think I would fare against the greatest tennis player of all time, Rafael Nadal?

If you said, "Not particularly well," then you are being far too kind. I would get crushed.

Let's try and make things more fair.

What if I trot out onto the court equipped with a state-of-the-art racket and we give Rafa something off the shelf from Walmart? How do you like my chances now?

That's right, I'm still going to get crushed. There's simply too much of a skill disparity. The racket is inconsequential.

It's the same thing in real estate. The operator is the most important part of any deal.

Many new investors fixate on the specifics of a deal (a.k.a. the racket). They overvalue the projected returns, the proformas, and the business plan. It makes sense why they do this, but it's all wrong.

A great operator can salvage a mediocre deal. A bad operator will ruin an otherwise great deal.

Rafael Nadal could probably beat me in a game of tennis with nothing more than a wooden spoon. It doesn't matter how great of a racket you give me, I'm going to lose.

Your goal as a passive investor is to find the Rafael Nadals of apartment syndications, the guys and gals who are so good that they're going to deliver exceptional results no matter what.

So here's the million-dollar question: **How do you find the right team?**

Well, in our book, to sufficiently vet a deal sponsor, you need to know five things: their personality, track record, team, education, and trustworthiness.

5 TRAITS TO LOOK FOR IN AN OPERATOR

Personality:

> *"You're not wrong, Walter, you're just an asshole."*
>
> — The Big Lebowski

No, you aren't looking for charm and charisma. That would be akin to buying a car from the guy with the best smile. You're looking for an operator who views the world the same way you do. An operator who shares your goals, values, and investment thesis.

Are they inherently optimistic and seeking massive returns while you're more conservative and seeking steady, incremental progress?

Are they detail-oriented or a big-picture dreamer? If you're a detail person who likes a well-articulated plan and regular updates, then you might not appreciate the type of operator who has their head higher in the clouds.

How does this operator communicate? Does it align with how you prefer to receive information? We all communicate differently. You don't want to leave a conversation with your partner feeling more confused than when it began. This isn't to say that these people are bad communicators. It might just be that the two of you don't communicate on the same wavelength.

Personality alignment can be a hard thing to nail down. If you've ever interviewed somebody for a job or been on a first date, you know how difficult this step can be.

So to that we say, take your time and ease into the relationship. Spend a little extra time on the phone or grabbing a coffee. Make certain you really want to work with this person and that, above all, you can trust them.

Never rush into a deal or partnership.

"Play long-term games with long-term people."

— Naval Ravikant

It can take a long time of simply observing how a person moves through the world before you become comfortable enough to work with them. Don't be afraid to give yourself that necessary time.

Three traits we look for in every partner: **Are they smart, hardworking, and do they have integrity?**

"Smart" in this context doesn't mean inherent intelligence. It's about their knowledge of what they do. They should be masters of their craft.

There are plenty of brilliant, lazy people in the world. Doesn't mean we want to work with them. Hard work is the most important variable of success and it's non-negotiable.

If you partner with a smart, hardworking crook, then on a long enough time frame, they will cheat you out of your money.

Find a partner with the right combination of smarts, work ethic, and integrity, and you'll be hard-pressed to go wrong.

Track Record:

> *"Experience is simply the name we give our mistakes."*
>
> — Oscar Wilde

Verifying a sponsor's track record is far easier than verifying their personality. Success doesn't happen in a vacuum. It leaves clues. The same goes for failure.

If there's no trail, well, that kind of tells you something, doesn't it?

Now, when reviewing a sponsor's track record, don't be blinded by impressive returns on their past projects. Past performance doesn't guarantee future performance. It's more important to focus on what *drove* that success and whether those factors are replicable on future deals.

Ask questions about deals that failed to live up to expectations and how the sponsor reacted. We invariably learn more from our failures than our successes. It's "trial and error," not "trial and success." There's nothing wrong with failing.

> *"It is possible to commit no mistakes and still lose. That is not a weakness. That is life."*

> — Jean-Luc Picard

In asking about failures, you want to see *how* the operator responds. Do they claim personal responsibility for mistakes or do they point fingers at external sources (people, events, market cycles, etc.)?

Most important of all, what did they learn and how have they adapted their systems as a result?

Let's not lose sight of the fact that there are black swan events beyond anyone's control. The COVID pandemic took a lot of great operators (in many industries) completely off guard and wiped them out. The question isn't, "How could they be so stupid?" it's, "If you could do it again, knowing what you know now, what would you do differently?"

Pro Tip: *Don't just look at how previous deals performed. Look at how they performed relative to the original business plan. Did the operator project a 20% IRR, but only deliver 17%? That's not a terrible return, but it's suspicious when compared with the original objective.*

Avoid operators who over-promise and under-deliver. It's only a matter of time until they fail to deliver at all.

Not all operators have taken a deal full cycle (meaning they've seen a project through all the way to completion). New operators might lack this valuable marker of success. That's not necessarily a bad thing. Everybody starts somewhere.

Some of the best syndicators of the future are cutting their teeth today. Should you pass on them while they hone their skills? Maybe, maybe not.

For us, it comes down to previous career and experiences. Some skills and experiences are worth more than others.

A kindergarten teacher might lack some relevant underwriting skills when compared to a financial analyst. A computer programmer might not have much experience overseeing a team of contractors compared to a business owner with years of project management experience.

Weigh a new syndicator's potential to execute the deal against their past experiences. Regardless of field, all-stars rise to the top of whatever they do. Look for somebody who was the "best" at whatever they did before.

Excellence is a habit.

Team:

> *"None of us is as smart as all of us."*
>
> — Ken Blanchard

Apartment syndications are a "we" game, not a "me" game.

Your operator might be the best thing since sliced bread, but they can't manage every aspect of a deal on their own. You can tell a lot about the potential success of a syndication from the team assembled around the general partners.

In addition to the deal sponsors, some key professional partners are the property management company, contractors, lenders, lawyers, and any individuals serving in an advisory capacity.

If the operator lacks experience, it becomes even more imperative that they're surrounded by a strong team that's motivated to see the project succeed.

When executing the value-add business model, pay particularly close attention to the property management team.

The property management team will be on the property every single day executing the business plan. This makes them one of the most important aspects of a deal. Ensure the deal sponsors have partnered with the right team and that they're not cutting corners by simply going with the cheapest option.

There are many types of property management companies in this space, each with their own core competencies and experience. Finding the right team to run the deal is critical.

Some property managers focus on single-family housing and condos. Others focus on stabilized Class A apartment complexes.

These groups might be fantastic in their niches, but if you're entering into a fifty-unit Class C value-add project centered around heavy renovations and upgrading the resident pool, then both of the aforementioned groups might lack the skills and expertise to execute the business model.

Ask your deal sponsor why they selected the property management company they did, how their current portfolio looks, and why they're the right fit for that deal in particular.

Education and Resourcefulness:

> *"It's not about your resources, it's about your resourcefulness."*

> — Tony Robbins

Whether new or more experienced, your operator should have a deep knowledge of the market, deal structures, risk, and financing options.

Ideally, they have some form of online presence or thought leadership platform (with videos, blog articles, and podcasts) so you can dive deep into their thoughts and expertise. Also, operators with an online presence have more skin in the game in the form of reputational risk. If nobody knows your operator, then they don't stand to lose any of their nonexistent reputation if a deal goes south.

Reputation takes years to build and only a minute to lose. It's nice to work with operators who've spent those years building a reputation.

In a coming section, we provide an in-depth list of questions to ask a potential operator. Here are a few quick ones for assessing their knowledge and resources:

- *What do you love about this deal? What concerns you? How do you plan to mitigate those concerns?*

- *Where or who will you turn to if things go sideways?*

- *Have you worked with property managers, tenants, and local government agencies in the past?*

These questions are all designed to help you answer the question: **Does my operator know what they're doing and are they resourceful enough to protect my money?**

Additionally, you want to learn how this operator reacts when things don't go according to plan.

Do they double down on communication and face the problem head-on, or do they put their head in the sand and point fingers at everything outside of their control? Do they prioritize their investor's best interest or their own?

Investing is inherently risky. If you stay in the game long enough, you'll experience setbacks, failures, and difficulties. We are only human and can't expect perfection. What we can expect is a clear plan of action for how operators will handle unexpected circumstances.

Trustworthiness:

> *"Whoever is careless with the truth in small matters*
> *cannot be trusted with important matters."*

— Albert Einstein

Trustworthiness is hard to assess. Somebody's true character isn't something you'll discover during a ten-minute conversation. And yet, it's the most important thing to look for.

Often, you might have nothing more to go off of than a gut feeling or a niggling voice in the back of your head. Doubts are natural. You're entrusting this person with your hard-earned life savings. Take your time through this period and keep asking questions until you're satisfied and comfortable moving forward.

To determine that a person's trustworthy, we have to understand their motivations and goals. What are their long-term plans? Why do they get out of bed every morning? Why, of all the paths they could have chosen through life, did they land on this one?

Most people won't tell you truthfully if they intend to screw you over. If they do, well, I suppose that makes them trustworthy, though probably not somebody you should work with.

Spend the necessary time learning about the sponsor's underlying motivations and values. Remember, apartment syndications are illiquid investment vehicles that are held for between three and ten years on average. That's a long time to be in a relationship. Time invested on the front end will save you heartache in the long run.

Additionally, it's never a bad idea to run a background check on a prospective sponsor. Of course, operators are legally required to disclose past felonies, though that doesn't mean they will. Due diligence is your responsibility. If you hop into bed with somebody with a public history of malfeasance and you don't catch it because you skipped this step, well, I'm afraid you have nobody to blame but yourself.

A couple resources for running background checks are TLO.com and trustify.com.

References are nice, but in our experience, if you ask to speak to somebody currently invested in a sponsor's deal, they'll likely connect you with one of their raving fans. I've yet to ever speak to a reference who didn't give a glowing endorsement.

Here's a better idea: Ask to speak to the sponsor's professional contacts. Lenders, property management companies, brokers, and contractors have nothing to gain by sugarcoating the truth or outright lying. Of course, the operator will refer you to contacts they're on good terms with. Still, these conversations can provide valuable insight into how the operator runs their business.

Do they communicate clearly and follow through in a timely fashion? Do they pay their bills on time? How's the quality of their work?

These are all simple questions to ask a professional contact and can provide valuable insight.

One last thing to consider: don't partner with an operator who looks at you and sees only a dollar sign.

Do they respect you and your investment goals? Do they take the time to answer your questions or do they shrug you off? Do you feel as though you're constantly being sold to?

Also, don't forget to ask if the sponsor is co-investing in the deal alongside the limited partners. It's not a deal breaker if they say no, but it's a valuable touch point to gauge the operator's ultimate commitment to the deal.

Why might a deal sponsor not co-invest?

Well, remember that the deal sponsors are responsible for signing on the loan. To fulfill this obligation, the sponsors must meet certain liquidity and net worth requirements. If they can't, they'll have to bring in a key principal (KP) to provide a strong personal balance sheet to guarantee the loan.

Regardless of whether they utilize a key principal, it's important for the deal sponsors to maintain a strong financial position, which often means they can't simply reinvest everything they have into the next deal.

With that said, it's our personal belief that sponsors should co-invest *something* in a deal. We sleep better at night knowing our deal sponsors have actual skin in the game.

BETTING ON THE JOCKEY

The right operator can turn a mediocre deal into a fantastic deal—whereas the wrong operator can take a great deal and flush it down the toilet, along with all your money.

Find a trustworthy operator whose personality and investment goals align with your own and who has a track record of success, a rock-star team of professionals, and deep knowledge and expertise. If you do, then the sky is the limit for your passive investing journey.

HOW SYNDICATORS MAKE MONEY

If you want to succeed in business (and life), pay attention to how the person sitting across from you stands to benefit from being there. If you know what's in it for them, then you can reverse engineer their motives and actions.

Learn why people do the things they do and you won't be surprised, frustrated, or disappointed when they do something you disagree with. At minimum, you'll understand *why* they did it.

Take online marketing gurus, for example. Many a social media advertising guru would have you believe they've unlocked the secret to increasing your business' revenue by 1,000% overnight. They've conveniently bundled this advertising silver bullet into an easy to consume three-part online course that'll only cost you $999.

So here's the question: **How does this person get paid?**

Well, if they *really* had the secret to increasing sales so dramatically, wouldn't they be best served actually utilizing said skill? There are no shortages of businesses out there willing to pay a pretty penny in exchange for a 1,000% increase in sales overnight, right? So why is this genius of advertising hawking an online course for $1,000 a pop?

Think on that.

> *"What you do speaks so loudly that*
> *I cannot hear what you're saying."*
>
> — Ralph Waldo Emerson

Watch what people do, not what they say. In the example of our marketing guru, his actions don't map to his words.

What's the point?

First, the world's full of unscrupulous individuals looking to make a quick buck off of you. Which isn't to say that all marketing gurus are evil or should be avoided. There are many reasons for doing things besides money. People aren't coin-operated, after all. Second, in the world of apartment syndications, find an operator who will work hard for the investment *and* for you.

This only occurs with proper fiscal alignment of interest between all parties. To that end, let's talk about how deal sponsors are typically compensated.

EQUITY SPLIT

Here's a quick recap of the equity split.

Limited partners and general partners are entitled to a percentage of the equity in a deal based upon a predetermined split. Most offerings split around 70/30 (with 70% going to the LPs and 30% to the GPs). The portion that general partners receive in exchange for their work is called the promote.

We've previously discussed how nuanced these structures can get, so we won't get overly thorough here. Just know that in an ideally structured deal, the majority of a sponsor's compensation should come by way of the equity split when selling a property.

Equity is the preferred way to compensate the general partnership because it ensures they see the deal through to completion. The better the project performs, the more money everybody in the deal makes.

FEES

Fees are the second way to compensate operators. Now, you might have some negative feelings toward fees, but they're necessary and, when applied correctly, don't adversely affect the deal.

Why are fees a necessary evil?

Well, think about it from the deal sponsor's perspective. If we structure our offering with a preferred return, then the majority of cash flow throughout the life of a project goes to the limited partners. If the only compensation a sponsor stands to earn is upon disposition, then they could theoretically go years before making any meaningful income.

The best operators are full-time in this business. I don't know about you, but it'd be hard for me to go up to five years without a payday. Fees keep the operator's lights on over the life of a project while also compensating them for all the work and risk they took in finding and acquiring the deal.

Many operators only do a single deal per year, although they're looking at dozens if not hundreds of opportunities. Throughout this process they are spending countless hours underwriting, touring properties, putting up risk capital, and doing all the myriad things necessary for eventually finding an opportunity.

If sponsors weren't compensated for all this activity, they'd simply stop. Without any deals on the table, everybody loses out. Fees are necessary, but they shouldn't be excessive.

Here are the most common fees to expect.

Acquisition Fee: (*1–4% of purchase price*)

This one-time fee is earned upon closing for all the time, money, and resources expended by the general partners in evaluating the property, organizing the funding, and closing the deal. Because the amount of work involved in acquiring a one-hundred-million-dollar building isn't exponentially different than acquiring a ten-million-dollar property, this fee percentage usually decreases as the purchase size of the deal increases.

Asset Management Fee: (*1-3% of effective gross income*)

This recurring fee compensates the sponsor for managing the asset over the life of the hold. Asset management tasks include executing the business plan, managing the property management team, disbursing ongoing distributions, filing taxes, legal paperwork, and more. This fee is recurring, so it's important you understand exactly how it's calculated.

The asset management fee is typically based on **effective gross income (EGI)**. This method makes the sponsor's fee proportional to how well the property performs. If rent collections take a dip, so does the asset management fee. We prefer this method of establishing the asset management fee because it pegs compensation to performance, whereas many of the other ways of calculating the asset management fee do not.

For example, the fee could be based on the purchase price or amount of equity raised. In these structures, the fee is pegged to a static number, regardless of the property's performance. Needless to say, we don't like it when sponsors earn big compensation regardless of how well they perform.

Loan Guarantee Fee: *(1% or less of total loan amount)*

An individual with a strong balance sheet and sufficient liquidity needs to be on the loan regardless of whether the loan is recourse or non-recourse. If the sponsors lack the financial strength to guarantee the loan themselves, they'll bring in a key principal. This high-net-worth individual lends their balance sheet and, in exchange for the risk incurred, they receive a one-time fee of around 1% of the total loan amount.

Refinance Fee/Bonus: *(0.5–1% of new loan amount)*

Everybody loves a good refinance. It returns a significant portion of investor capital and signifies the deal is performing well. The refinance fee is an incentive hurdle for hitting certain metrics and returning a predetermined portion of capital.

Disposition Fee: *(1% of sale price)*

Selling an apartment building isn't like selling a single-family home. It can take months to prepare a property, the paperwork, and financial records for a sale. The disposition fee is a one-time compensation for all the work involved in exiting an asset.

These are only a few of the most common fees. There are countless others. Every operator is different, so be sure to ask questions so you fully understand all the fees, when they trigger, and for how much.

Whenever possible, seek performance-based incentives that are based on the successful execution of the business plan. Predatory fees occur regardless of the asset's performance. Sponsors who are well-compensated regardless of how the deal performs are not encouraged to deliver exceptional results. Those aren't sponsors we're keen to work with.

QUESTIONS TO ASK

You will face no decision more important in your passive investing career than the one you make regarding which operators to work with. Bad operators destroy good deals. Great operators *create* great deals.

Remember, the difference between a one-million-dollar idea and one million dollars is roughly one million dollars' worth of execution. Always vote for the guy or gal who can execute, not the one with the shiniest idea.

Here are some key questions to ask potential operators to discover if there's an alignment of personality, a track record of success, a team of rock stars, and underlying trustworthiness.

Track Record

- How many deals have you closed? How many have you taken full cycle?

- What were the actual returns compared to the projected performance? May I look at the marketing materials for your past deals?

- Tell me about a deal that didn't go to plan. How did you handle it? What caused the issue? What would you do differently?

Experience

- How many assets do you currently have under management?

- How long have you been investing in real estate?

- How did you get started in real estate investing?

- Why this particular niche and business plan?

- How many assets of this type do you have in this particular market?

- Have you ever failed to hit projected returns? If so, why?

Team

- Who are the major players on your team?

- What are their backgrounds? What are their roles? What experience do they have in their roles?

- How did you meet the other members of your team?

- How long have you known them?

- Have you ever had a partnership fail? If so, what happened?

- When I run a background and credit check, what will I find?

- Why are you working with these partners in particular?

Compensation

- Are you investing in the deal? If so, how much? If not, why not?

- What fees (and how much) do you charge?

- Acquisition fee

- Guarantor fee

- Asset management fee

- Refinance/disposition fee

- Others?

- Why those fees and those percentages in particular?

- If the deal fails to perform, do you still collect your fees?

- In what ways do you create alignment of interest with your passive investors?

Trustworthiness

- What were your three biggest concerns with your last deal? Why those three? What did you do to mitigate them?

- Have you experienced these concerns or issues before? How did you deal with them?

- If everything went sideways, what would you do?

- How do you view losing your investor's money?

- Have you ever lost your investor's money or had to do a capital call? If so, what happened?

- What would you do if facing the possibility of losing your investor's money?

- In what ways do you consider the underwriting on your last deal to be conservative or optimistic? Why do you believe that to be the case?

- Can you show me exactly where you've been conservative and where you've been optimistic?

- Do you have alternative models you can show me with different levels of sensitivity analysis? What are the worst, expected, and best-case outcomes of your last deal?

- Have you ever been sued? If so, why?

EVEN PASSIVE INVESTORS MUST NETWORK

I'm an introvert with hermit-like tendencies. Networking is just about the most difficult thing in the world for me. In the beginning of my real estate investing career, I forced myself to attend meet-ups and networking events. Unfortunately, the moment the educational portion of the presentation finished, I'd run for the door.

That's right, I went to networking events and bailed before the *actual* networking began.

They say 90% of success in life is just showing up. Then again, 80% of all statistics are made up, so take that with a grain of salt. Regardless of whether the math checks out, there's a lot of truth in that nugget of wisdom.

I technically accomplished the showing up part. Of course, I didn't stay long, but that's beside the point. Eventually I became more comfortable in these strange new environments with these strange new people.

Time and familiarity breed confidence. To all of you painfully shy introverts scared at the thought of walking into a room of strangers and striking up a conversation, I say this: *just show up.*

Take one small step after another beyond the edge of your comfort zone and one day you'll look back to be surprised at just how much your comfort zone has expanded. I share my networking struggles with the hope that it connects with those of you who want to invest in real estate but who are petrified by the idea of putting themselves out there. In many ways it feels like high school all over again.

With all that said, here are some thoughts on the subject of networking so you can get the most out of meet-ups, conferences, and simple one-on-one phone calls.

But wait...

Aren't you a *passive* investor? Why should any of this matter to you?

Because to participate in an apartment syndication you have to, at minimum, know an operator.

That's not to say you *must* attend meet-ups and conferences. The internet is a powerful tool for connecting with operators from all over the world, but at some point you'll have to hop on a call with someone, and what is that if not micro-networking?

What follows are some tidbits for maximizing the value you get from meeting strangers (whether that be on the phone or in person).

DON'T FAKE IT TILL YOU MAKE IT

Somehow this little piece of advice has become incredibly pervasive in the world of business and investing. Many people simply accept it at face value without thinking deeply about it.

Part of this advice is rooted in the pseudoscientific belief that you can manifest your destiny by speaking your desires out into the universe.

Don't get me wrong, I do affirmations every morning and I believe strongly in the power of visualizing successful outcomes, but there's a difference between:

"I am worthy and deserving of money, wealth is my birthright. Money flows easily to me. My financial freedom is only one step away. It is flowing to me. I can feel it."

And...

"I am a man of knowledge and execution. I do not simply think about acting. I choose my path with conviction and follow it with discipline."

One of these sets a clear intention followed by distinct actions... the other screams into the void that you're a special little butterfly, and then sits back and hopes for the best.

Here's my problem with "fake it 'till you make it": you're new and, with the exception of the other newbies, you won't fool anybody. Especially the people you *want* to work with.

Stay authentic.

Own the fact that you're new. Use it as an opportunity to ask questions and learn. People love helping people; it gives them a sense of purpose. Allow yourself to be helped, and you'll be surprised how people rally around you.

DON'T BE A COMPLETE BEGINNER

There's a seemingly infinite supply of educational books, videos, podcasts, webinars, and courses floating around the internet (and many of these things are even free!) The places you shouldn't go looking for an introductory education, however, are meet-ups, networking events, and conferences. These events typically contain an educational component, though you'd be wise to treat this as continuing education rather than establishing fundamentals.

Why should you avoid meet-ups before you've established a baseline knowledge? Two reasons.

First, these events are frequented by busy professionals who are actively seeking mutually beneficial relationships within an established niche. It's incredibly difficult to help somebody who doesn't yet know enough about the industry to even know where they want to focus.

Second, start with the end in mind. If you're planning to go into an event with a "let's see what happens" attitude, I'll just save you the trip now. Here's what will happen: not much.

So that's ground zero. Before you attend any meet-up, at least know enough to have identified which real estate investing niche you're interested in pursuing. Once you've identified your niche (passive investing in multifamily real estate syndications, for example), determine your objective in attending the event.

If you show up with those two things dialed in, you're likely to leave that event finding exactly what you were looking for.

WHY THIS MATTERS

It might be surprising to learn that there's a *lot* of capital in the system looking for a great deal. In fact, there's an overall shortage of great deals out there.

Great operators (you know, the ones you want to work with) don't struggle to find the capital to fund their deals. If you want to work with these operators, it's your job to vet them, but realize that they're also vetting *you*.

It's paramount that you make a good first impression and present yourself as somebody *they* want to work with. Resist the shyness and insecurity. Be brave. Get out there and network.

You never know, the next great deal could be just one conversation away.

CHAPTER 12

EVALUATING MARKETS

"Every person who invests in well-selected real estate in a growing section of a prosperous community adopts the surest and safest method of becoming independent, for real estate is the basis of wealth."

— Theodore Roosevelt

Long-distance running is a special sort of hell. Some days the miles tick by so easily it almost feels like you're running down a hill with the wind at your back. Every long-distance runner eventually learns, however, that you'd better enjoy those downhills and tailwinds because there comes a point on every run when you have to turn around and head home.

Now you're running *up* the hills and that wind isn't doing you any favors.

Of course, if you wanted to, you could arrange it so you only ever run down the hills. Perhaps a caring friend or family member could pick you up in a car at the bottom of every hill. If all else fails, you could always call an Uber. But that would sort of defeat the purpose of running in the first place, wouldn't it? The challenge *is* the goal.

You're intentionally seeking out the difficulty so that your body is forced to adapt and improve. In many ways, long-distance running is a lesson in abject masochism.

It's not the same with real estate investing. No awards are given for making things harder than they need to be.

When it comes to real estate investing, we only ever want to run *down* the hills. And we most certainly do not want to struggle against any headwinds.

It's cliche but true: *real estate is all about location, location, location.*

With the right location, things get so much easier.

Location means a few different things ranging from the state, metropolitan statistical area (MSA), county, neighborhood, all the way down to the individual block level.

At the macro level, some cities present a better investment opportunity based on cost of housing, median income, job growth, unemployment rates, and demographic trends. Scaling down to the neighborhood level, it's important to understand the local economic, political, and cultural factors impacting the quality of schools, crime levels, proximity to amenities, and median income.

Passive investors should know how to analyze markets from a high level. The rest of this chapter will teach you how to do just that.

INVESTING LOCAL VERSUS OUT OF STATE

Many investors want the ability to physically see their property whenever the spirit moves them. That's one of the reasons we invest in the Twin

Cities. We're control freaks and like knowing we can be at our properties in under ten minutes if emergency strikes. As operators with in-house property management, this makes a lot of sense for us.

Passive investors benefit from the ability to participate in the wide variety of hot markets spread across the country. This leads to higher deal flow, allowing you to be more selective. The great weakness of diversification is the additional time it requires for analyzing each new market, sector, or operator.

Then again, looking remotely might be a necessary evil if you live in high-priced markets like San Francisco or New York City. It doesn't matter how well you know these markets, you're going to struggle to find a deal that actually makes sense.

Whether you choose to invest in your backyard or look across the country, the process of selecting a market doesn't have to be complicated. You don't have to memorize every detailed nuance of a market to be confident it's trending in the right direction. To that end, we're going to simplify the market selection process by focusing in on the key economic, regulatory, and local market factors that matter most.

ECONOMIC FACTORS

When it comes to real estate investing, we're looking for a solid macro-economic tailwind at the MSA level. This means wide economic diversity in the industries comprising the majority of an area's jobs. Detroit's economy in the 2000s was a one-trick pony (the automotive industry). When that pony got sick and had to be put down, the city crumbled alongside it.

So, when considering a potential market, you want to first identify the big economic players and whether they all swim in the same pool (industry). Ideally, we're looking for a good mix of Fortune 500 companies offering a wide variety of jobs across multiple sectors.

Where there's a strong economic foundation, there are jobs. Where there are jobs, there are people.

When it comes to evaluating a potential market, few things are more important than jobs and people. Without those, you have a city with a bleak outlook.

Strong job growth typically points to increasing wages, decreasing unemployment rates, and, overall, a higher standard of living for residents. These factors, when combined, create a melting pot of opportunity.

REGULATORY FACTORS

Some markets are friendlier to real estate investors than others. Be aware of this. State and local legislation can have a massive impact on the overall success of an investment.

Markets with excessively friendly tenant rights can prove difficult to operate within. Sometimes returns that can be generated in certain markets aren't worth the bureaucratic red tape and headache.

You're welcome to invest in markets with rent control, difficult eviction processes, and restrictive tenant screening, but you're willingly running *up* the hill and making things unnecessarily difficult.

LOCAL MARKET FACTORS

At the micro-neighborhood level, we want to evaluate overall neighborhood safety, quality of schools, access to public transportation, proximity to shopping and recreation, and density of competition.

Here are a couple of things we consider when looking at a neighborhood.

First, if we were thinking about renting an apartment, how would we feel about that neighborhood? Does it pass the "go for a walk alone after dark" test? If not, then it doesn't matter how rapidly the rest of the city grows, you'll struggle to find quality tenants willing to live in your building.

Second, is the property similar in quality to the rest of the neighborhood? In particular, avoid buying the nicest building on the block, unless you have good reasons to believe that that area will rapidly improve. On the other hand, it's hard to go wrong when you buy the worst building on the block. You'll realize some great appreciation if you can bring it into alignment with the rest of the neighborhood.

EIGHT-STEP EVALUATION PROCESS

There are many factors to consider when evaluating a potential market. Here's a simple eight-step process to help quickly vet a market starting from the top (macro-MSA) and working our way down to ground level (micro-neighborhood)

We'll utilize a couple online resources to aid in the analysis process, such as www.city-data.com and https://geomap.ffiec.gov/FFIECGeocMap/ GeocodeMap1.aspx. Yes, that's a weird URL, but trust me, it's a fantastic tool for sifting through census data.

Step 1: Population Growth

You can find most everything you need to vet a city at city-data.com. The first thing to look at when evaluating a market is population growth. A market with strong growth suggests that it's on the right side of the supply/demand curve. The more people flocking to a city, the more potential renters.

New buildings can only be constructed so quickly. Of those new buildings, generally it's cost-prohibitive to build affordable housing to compete with Class B and C properties. A crunch occurs when there's a cap on supply, but demand continues to grow. This leads to increasing rent, which leads to higher valuations, which in turn leads to favorable market conditions for investment.

Utilizing city-data.com, we want to consider how the population has grown in a particular MSA over the past twenty years and by how much. It's important to take the long view of population growth. Some cities have experienced explosive new growth, which signals a hot market worth consideration. At Invictus Capital, we prefer cities with a long history of high demand, which suggests solid underlying fundamentals.

What's considered good growth? Over a twenty-year window, consider 20% growth (about 1% per year) to be a solid baseline.

A quick note about cities with declining populations. During the pandemic of 2020, we saw an exodus from certain large metropolitan areas (San Francisco and New York, in particular). Does this mean these cities are doomed to collapse? Probably not.

There's a difference between people fleeing a city due to fear in the short term versus people draining away year over year because of a stagnating market (Detroit in the 2000s).

At the moment, it's too early to say what will happen with San Francisco or New York in the short term, but it's hard to bet against them in the long run. This isn't to suggest that these are desirable investment cities, of course. When vetting markets, dig for the second order consequences of macro-level events.

Step 2: Income Growth

With an increase in population, you would expect to see a corresponding growth in income. If that's not the case, then you could have a problem on your hands.

Think about what happens if a lot of people move into a city with stagnating income growth. Rent and cost of living will increase in response to the greater demand on a limited supply, but people's overall purchasing power will slowly erode. That's a recipe for disaster.

To look up a city's income growth, we again turn to city-data.com. For a point of reference, to keep pace with inflation since the year 2000, a city will need to have seen about 30% growth. If a city hasn't kept pace with inflation, then it's potentially facing some big issues in the years to come (if it hasn't already).

Step 3: Unemployment Rate

A simple Google search will return city and national unemployment rates. With those numbers in hand, we then use ffiec.gov to zero in on a particular neighborhood.

First, avoid MSAs with significantly higher unemployment rates (or upward-trending rates) compared to the national average. Second, avoid neighborhoods with an unemployment rate 2% higher than the city's average. These are the neighborhoods that get hit the hardest in a recession.

Step 4: Crime Levels

Crime levels become increasingly important at the neighborhood level. City police departments typically maintain robust statistics on local crime levels. This information unfortunately isn't always readily available. Sometimes you can find this information posted online, but often these reports are on macro-MSA crime levels.

To zero in on an individual neighborhood, try calling the local police department. Even if they won't share statistical data, they might share some anecdotal information that's equally valuable. Here's a great question to ask:

How many (and what sorts of) calls do you get in that area?

Getting a sense for a neighborhood's crime level is particularly important if you're an out-of-state investor lacking neighborhood-level insights.

Step 5: Neighborhood Household Income

The ffiec.gov is the best resource I've found for viewing street-by-street comparisons of median income. Median income helps determine whether there's a large enough pool of potential tenants capable of affording your product in a neighborhood.

This number fluctuates depending on market, but living expenses usually account for around 30% of a person's budget. A one-bedroom unit in the markets we target rent for about $1,000 per month. Somebody earning around $40,000 should be able to afford this. If the neighborhood household income is $28,000, on the other hand, then we might struggle to find enough qualified candidates.

Step 6: Neighborhood Poverty Level

Again, ffiec.gov provides granular data on poverty levels on a street-by-street basis. Anything above 20% is a red flag and you'll likely face an uphill battle to find reliable long-term residents in that particular neighborhood.

Step 7: Amenities

Take a quick virtual stroll around the block utilizing Google Street View to locate the nearest amenities including grocery stores, shopping, gas, restaurants, schools, and access to public transit lines. You can tell an awful lot about a neighborhood based on which stores you find.

If you see a Starbucks or Whole Foods, then you're probably in at least a Class B, if not A, area. Are there McDonald's, Walmarts, and payday loan centers every corner? Then you're probably not in the hottest up-and-coming neighborhood around.

MARKET REPORTS

Even passive investors should keep a finger on the pulse of the industry and market at large. Here are some free annual industry reports to keep an eye on.

Marcus & Millichap Annual U.S. Multifamily Investment Forecast: Here's a fantastic macro-level analysis of economic and political factors potentially affecting the multifamily niche in the coming year. This report also ranks the major U.S. real estate markets across a litany of factors. This is a great tool for spotting the best investment cities in the country.

Milken Index Best Cities Report: A non-profit think tank produces this report, and it's packed full of useful information. Milken creates a "Top 25 Best Cities" list based on an index measuring job growth, wage growth, short-term job growth, high-tech job growth, and more. You can expect impressive insights on each featured MSA.

Integra Realty Resources Annual Viewpoint Commercial Real Estate Trends Report: The name's a mouthful, but this top-notch data-driven report delivers incredible insight about how macro-level real estate trends might be affected by current economic and political events.

CBRE Biannual Cap Rate Survey: Passive investors will find this report a bit in the weeds, but it offers strong insight into market cap rates and expected returns, which helps establish investment baselines when considering new markets. If I were to invest in a city I was unfamiliar with, I'd have no sense for the current market trading conditions. This report helps illuminate how conservative or aggressive an operator's underwriting assumptions might be for an area.

COMPLETING YOUR MARKET RESEARCH

Through your market research, you're trying to identify markets capable of thriving in both the good times and the bad. Invest in cities and neighborhoods with strong fundamentals, and you'll rarely be disappointed should the market take an unexpected dip.

CHAPTER 13

BUILDING YOUR TEAM

"If you want to go fast, go alone. If you want to go far, go together."

— African Proverb

Dan admits he had a bit of an ego problem when he first started his real estate investing journey. In everything he did, he wanted to be able to say, "I did that."

There's a deep pride and satisfaction in building something by yourself. And so, in the beginning, Dan resisted the idea of partnerships and did everything himself.

Most entrepreneurs experience this "Ima Mentality" at some point.

I'ma do this...

I'ma do that...

I'ma do it all...

Often people get into entrepreneurship and building businesses because there's a bit of a maverick in them that resists answering to others. While it's understandable to operate from this mindset, it can be short-sighted and limiting.

Successful multifamily investors know real estate is a "we" game, not a "me" game. There are so many moving parts throughout an apartment syndication that it's simply impractical for a single person to do it all.

Obviously, passive investors by definition rely on the efforts of others to succeed. Less obvious are which roles you need filled on your team, and, most difficult of all, how do you find the right person?

So let's first break down some of the most important roles you'll need to fill on your personal team (personal lawyer, CPA, operators, mentor). After you have your team good to go, we'll turn our attention to some of the roles you'll want to see on your general partner's team (property management company, contractors, SEC attorney, lender, mentor).

First, a note about expenses. All the roles on your team are designed to make you more money than they cost you. Don't cut corners by thinking you can do without one of these roles or by simply going with whoever is cheapest.

LAWYER

Syndications are heavy on legal contracts. At various points you'll be faced with a stack of papers filled written in legalese (operating agreement, private placement memorandum (PPM), etc.). These are dense, legally-binding contracts designed to chalk the field and define the rules by which everybody's playing the game.

Your lawyer will find unfavorable clauses in these documents to make sure you're protected (or at least aware of all the risks associated). You should read these documents yourself, but unless you're a lawyer, you probably lack the skill to catch all the nuances.

One word changed in a single clause could affect the entire outcome of your investment. Don't leave this to chance and don't be stingy thinking you'll save a couple hundred dollars by doing it yourself or just trusting the operator.

CPA

A good CPA will save you more money than they cost. A bad CPA might land you in deep water.

Be certain your CPA has experience with real estate (and preferably syndications). Finding a CPA with deep domain experience in real estate will save you incredible amounts of money.

Believe it or not, Uncle Sam doesn't want you to pay more than you're obligated. Of course, the government won't go out of their way to catch mistakes that aren't in their favor, but that's beside the point.

The labyrinthine tax code, in its constantly evolving complexity, is beyond any single person's comprehension. This means that, quite often, finding yourself on the right side of the tax-man comes down to your *documentation* and the *story* justifying your decisions.

Most CPAs are, by nature, risk-averse creatures utterly lacking in creativity. A creative CPA willing to work on advanced strategies and tactics to minimize your liabilities is a godsend. If you find one of these mythical beasts, do whatever it takes to keep them around.

Avoid CPAs who get *too* creative, though. Stay on the right side of the law and pay Uncle Sam what's owed. Just be certain you aren't paying more.

It should go without saying, but once again, I'm not your legal or tax adviser, so take everything I say with a grain of salt.

OPERATOR

I think we've beaten this horse sufficiently by now, yes?

MENTOR/ADVISER

It's hard to overstate the value of this often-overlooked team member. With that said, not all mentors are created the same. You need a mentor experienced in apartment syndications or real estate in general. This mentor might be a fellow passive investor, or they could be an active operator. There's value in both.

The power of a mentor is that they've been where you are now and can steer you clear of common mistakes, thereby lessening the chance you do something stupid. You need somebody you can turn to with questions and fears.

Now, finding the right mentor can be tricky. The three best places to look are online forums, in-person meet-ups, and referrals.

Of the three, referrals are the most valuable, so start there.

Follow the networking principles laid out earlier when attending live events and, for the love of all that's sacred, do not, under any circumstance, *ask* somebody to be your mentor the first, second, or even third time you meet them.

That's no different than walking into a bar and asking the first woman you see if they'll marry you. To attract a good mate, you must first *become* a good mate.

Okay, enough dating advice. Good luck out there in both love and investing. Let's get back to real estate.

THE DEAL SPONSOR'S TEAM

Now that you've assembled your personal team, let's meet some of the members of the deal sponsor's team.

Property Management Company

It's hard to overstate the importance of this role. A million-dollar idea is worthless without million-dollar execution.

The property management company is the boots on the ground executing the business plan. They're the ones interacting with residents, contractors, maintenance personnel, and vendors to ensure the property performs up to expectation.

Some operators (like Invictus Capital) build out a separate property management company to handle their in-house management needs. This creates more work for us and isn't without downside, but we prefer this strategy because it gives us control over the quality of our customer service, our expenses, and ultimately the returns we're able to deliver to investors.

Most operators outsource property management to third-party companies. This also has its pros and cons. On the positive side, presumably you're working with experts who are great at what they do. This frees up the sponsors to focus time and energy elsewhere (such as on finding the next deal). Also, by outsourcing management, these operators aren't tied to a single market or asset class. They have the flexibility to pursue opportunities wherever they have connections with a quality property management team.

The downside, however, can be summarized by the classic principal-agent problem. This problem, at its core, revolves around the fact that it doesn't matter how much you pay the babysitter, nobody will love and care for your child more than you. Creating an incentive structure that produces strong alignment of interest between the agent (contractor/employee) and the principal (owner) is incredibly difficult.

There's no right or wrong way to handle property management. Both in-house and outsourced can be effective. In either scenario, here are the questions you'll need to answer:

Does the property management company have experience with similar assets?

If you're looking to acquire a fifty-unit apartment but the property management company primarily manages single-family homes, then they might not be a great fit.

Does the property management company have experience executing similar business plans?

Not all business plans are created equal. Some assets require a heavy renovation coupled with a complete turn of a less-than-desirable tenant base. Other assets might only require a little lipstick and rent bump. Be certain the property management company has both the ability and experience executing similar business plans to the one your sponsors intend to implement.

Contractors

A number of contractors will make an appearance throughout the life of a project. Those roles include inspectors, engineers, architects, and appraisers.

You don't need to vet every single one of these entities. Simply consider how the GP plans to fill these positions. Do they have prior relationships with all the necessary contractors or will they be turning to Yelp?

This matters. An operator brings value to the equation through their time, knowledge, experience, and *relationships*. A sponsor with no relationships is a bad sign.

Lawyers

Syndications require everybody to jump through a few more legal hoops than just a traditional operating agreement. Two types of lawyers are typically required: a general-purpose lawyer for all the things related to the transaction itself (title, negotiations, etc.) and another that specializes in SEC-related private placements.

Registering a private placement requires a litany of documents that are both expensive and specific. A general-purpose lawyer probably lacks the requisite experience to handle this well.

From drafting the operating and subscription agreement all the way to the private placement memorandum (PPM), this isn't the time nor the place to skimp on expenses by hiring your cousin's divorce attorney. Avoid any operator downloading boilerplate contracts from the internet. Cutting those corners almost guarantees they won't be in business long.

Commercial Lender

Here's a good rule for business and life: *follow the money*.

Even though you won't sign the loan or work directly with the bank, it's important to understand the bank, credit union, or other financial institution financing the project. You want to see a strong relationship between the GP and lending entity so you can be certain the deal won't fall apart in the eleventh hour.

Debt is so important that we'll dedicate an entire chapter to it shortly.

Asset Manager

One of the sponsors will most likely fill the role of asset manager, so you should have already vetted them. This person will oversee the entire project. They'll manage the property management company and ensure the deal stays on track, while also coordinating quarterly distributions and tax-related paperwork.

With that said, some groups outsource this responsibility to a third-party company specializing in asset management. We're personally not keen to outsource this critical position.

Adviser/Mentor

In the same way we recommend *you* have a mentor/adviser, it's reassuring to know that your sponsors have somebody they can turn to for advice. Think of it like a personal board of directors.

This isn't a must-have, but it's nice knowing the GP has access to the advice and support of another accomplished operator in the field.

DON'T UNDERESTIMATE THIS STEP

Dan eventually made the mental shift in how he thought about partnerships and came to realize that nobody thinks less of Steve Jobs because he had Steve Wozniak.

In our first year working together, Dan and I tripled the size of our portfolio, launched two podcasts, and wrote a book. The synergies in finding the *right* partner simply can't be measured. This is a game where you bet on the jockey, not the horse, after all.

Sure, there's a symbiotic relationship between the two, but all-star jockeys don't get on lame horses. Whether it be a CPA, lawyer, or deal sponsor, you need to find all-star jockeys for each role on the team.

People make the deal. Don't skimp on the process or outsource your judgment for the sake of expediency.

Take your time, expend the energy, and surround yourself with all-stars. If you do, it's only a matter of time until you're winning championships together.

CHAPTER 14

FINDING THE MONEY

"You are, at this moment, standing right in the middle of your own 'acres of diamonds."

— Earl Nightingale

For every reason there is to get started in real estate investing, there's an equal number of reasons (or excuses) for why people don't. Here's the most common excuse: *"I don't have enough money."*

True, if you want to passively invest in real estate, you need money, but in our experience, people have access to more capital than they even realize. One of the things that makes real estate investing so powerful is your ability to use other people's money.

In other words, **partners** and **leverage**.

Leverage enables us to acquire valuable assets without committing equivalent amounts of capital. A mortgage is a particularly powerful form of leverage. With bank financing, we only need to come to the closing table with around 25% of an asset's purchase price.

Now, that can still be a lot of money, and it begs the question: **Where do we come up with all of that?**

Well, by now you understand that the syndication model allows a group of investors to pool their time, knowledge, and capital to purchase large assets an individual investor couldn't acquire on their own. If we're purchasing an asset worth $10,000,000 and we need $2,500,000 to close, then instead of bringing all that money ourselves, we can partner with fifty investors, each bringing $50,000.

While $50,000 is a whole lot less than $2,500,000, it's still not an insignificant sum of money for most people. If you're staring at your savings account and thinking that maybe you wasted your time reading this far, don't worry. There are countless creative ways to summon the necessary funds to participate in a real estate syndication.

It might seem a daunting task, but let's not fixate on the problem. Let's spend our energy searching for solutions. Put another way, don't look for why you *can't* do a thing. Look for the reasons why you *can*. Or, more importantly, *how* you can.

Okay, so now that you're all fired up, let's explore four lesser-known places savvy investors can find the capital necessary to fund a deal.

Quick disclaimer: Chat with your legal and tax professional before making any decisions that could affect your personal financial situation. We're not your adviser, nor are we offering advice. This is purely for informational purposes only.

LIFE INSURANCE

Most people don't really understand life insurance. For instance, did you know you can borrow against the equity in your life insurance plan and use that money for... pretty much anything?

A recently opened account probably doesn't carry significant value, but if the account has been open for a number of years (perhaps you were the recipient of a policy as a wee child), then there might be a serious amount of equity sitting there waiting to be deployed.

Dan bought his first property utilizing this strategy. He leveraged his wife's life insurance plan to acquire his first six-unit apartment building. Nine months later, he refinanced that building, pulled out the majority of his capital, and redeployed it into the next property.

It's a powerful strategy requiring only a bit of savvy to properly execute.

SELF-DIRECTED IRA

The powerful tax-deferred advantages afforded by the Roth IRA make it a great investment vehicle. Unfortunately, in its typical configuration, you can only invest in a limited variety of traditional vehicles (e.g. stocks, bonds, etc.). If you want to invest in real estate, you're just out of luck, right?

Wrong.

Most people don't realize there's a simple way to invest their IRA funds into private real estate placements. Here are the caveats.

First, the funds must be in a self-directed IRA, which allows you to invest in all sorts of alternative vehicles such as alpacas, collectibles, and real estate, for example.

Second, you can't fund your *own* deal. Sorry, you can't pull money out to buy yourself a house (even for investment purposes). The money has to be deployed in *somebody else's* deal.

Which is where operators like us come in. Many of the investors participating in our offerings do so through self-directed IRAs. This powerful investment strategy simply rolls distributions from cash flow and capital events right back into the IRA, allowing you to realize long-term, tax-free compounded growth.

With that said, be aware that if you go down this road, you'll be subject to UBIT (Unrelated Business Income Tax). Despite this tax, the numbers still work out in favor of investing in real estate. Be sure to run through this scenario with your CPA so you're aware of all the implications and liabilities.

401(K) AND QUALIFIED RETIREMENT PLAN (QRP)

Another lesser-known source of capital comes from a different retirement account most working professionals likely have sitting around: the 401(k). Specifically a 401(k) from a *former* employer.

There are a couple ways you can do this.

First, you could take out a loan from the 401(k). The fundamentals are similar to using your life insurance policy. Speak to your tax adviser about the implications of utilizing this tactic, but in a pinch, this might be a great way to summon extra capital you never realized you had at your disposal.

Second, if you want to dive in with both feet, you could follow in Dan's footsteps and cash out all your retirement accounts. Be aware, however, that you'll get hit hard with significant fees and penalties that make this, all told, not the best option.

You'll have to run the numbers on that for yourself and in conjunction with your CPA (remember, we're not tax professionals and are not giving tax advice!). It made sense for Dan because he understood the opportunity cost of not jumping into real estate and deemed the rewards far superior to the potential losses.

So far, it seems he wasn't wrong.

Third, you could roll a 401(k) from a previous employer into a self-directed IRA, as in the previous example. Unfortunately, 401(k)s held by a current employer are unlikely to allow you to utilize this option.

If you have a solo 401(k), you are positioned to deploy your capital through a retirement fund *without* being subject to UBIT. This is an incredible strategy for those able to thread the needle. If you think this might be you, speak to your CPA about the qualified retirement plan.

HOME EQUITY LINE OF CREDIT (HELOC)

Last, but not least, we have the HELOC, or home equity line of credit.

The majority of most Americans' net worth exists in the form of equity in their primary residence. This makes sense. If you've lived in your primary residence for more than a couple years, then hopefully your property has experienced some appreciation coupled with a healthy amount of debt paydown.

HELOCs are a great short-term option. The interest rates typically fluctuate between 1 and 2% above prime with an interest-only payment structure over the term of the loan. This makes the HELOC great for quick fix-and-flip-style projects that'll only last six months to a year.

If you're eyeballing something longer than one year, you might be better off considering a home equity loan.

Many newer investors are on a mission to pay down the entirety of their mortgages. Sophisticated investors, on the other hand, realize the power of using other people's money (a.k.a. the bank) to purchase cash-flow-generating assets. Remove leverage from the equation and real estate still performs on par with the stock market, but you've really taken away one of the key factors making this investment vehicle so darn powerful.

Here are two key concepts to help you establish and maintain a healthy relationship with debt.

1. Use Debt to Buy Assets, Not Liabilities

Most people use debt to subsidize lifestyles they can't afford. They ring up expensive purchases and exotic vacations on a credit card in a compulsion to *keep up with the Joneses*. This is not only a perfect recipe for financial suicide, but also a great way to guarantee you spend your life in a state of discontent.

When we talk about using debt, we're not talking about consumer debt used to buy *toys*. We're talking about using debt to purchase cash-flow-generating assets that put money back in our pockets.

If you're new to this concept, I recommend that, immediately after completing this book, you go and pick up a copy of the iconic purple book: *Rich Dad, Poor Dad* by Robert Kiyosaki.

Judging by the fact that you're here, reading a book about passive investing, I'm going out on a limb and guessing you understand the power of good debt.

2. Don't Over-Leverage Yourself

Many were caught up in irrational exuberance during 2008's financial crisis. They were floating up to their eyeballs in debt and, when that final storm came, it sank them.

We're not suggesting you leverage yourself to the hilt, but it might be worth taking a look at your current financial situation and, if you're sitting on significant equity in your primary residence, you might ask yourself:

What is my ROE?

Return on Equity, the lesser-known cousin of Return on Investment (ROI), is the more nuanced way of thinking about the capital you have working for you in the world.

If hundreds of thousands of dollars' worth of equity exists in your primary residence, you should ask yourself whether that's truly the highest and best use of that money. Could that capital generate a better return if redeployed elsewhere?

If you answered yes, then give deep consideration to what you should do next. Investors who keep one eye on ROI and another on ROE understand how to maximize the velocity of their capital.

Now, you might value the safety and stability of knowing you have reduced liability. Investors more concerned with preserving capital than in growing capital might opt to stay the course.

We're not suggesting you use any of these options to fund a deal. Remember, investing is inherently risky. Regardless of which strategy you employ, make certain you fully understand the associated risks and rewards.

PART FIVE

EVALUATING DEALS

CHAPTER 15

METRICS

EVALUATING DEALS

*"Give me a lever long enough and a place to
stand and I will move the earth."*

— Archimedes

Many people love the idea of passive income because they think it means
they don't have to do any work. Don't misunderstand, limited partners
do a whole lot less work than deal sponsors, but successful passive investors don't throw their money at an operator and then sit back in the
comfort of expected returns.

No, successful passive investors know they have two important jobs:

1. Vet the sponsor

2. Vet the deal

That's less difficult than actually operating a deal, but it's not nothing.

Passive investors are required to do *some work*. Thankfully it's neither difficult nor time-consuming. Once you've completed the initial legwork and understand your investment parameters, you'll know almost instantly whether a potential deal is right for you.

The quickest way to this nirvana-like place of competence and confidence comes from understanding the key return terms and metrics upon which every deal hinges: cash-on-cash return, internal rate of return, annualized average return, preferred return, and equity multiple.

CASH-ON-CASH RETURN (COC)

The annualized returns relative to the initial amount invested.

This is the most common return metric investors consider. It's a simple way to quickly identify how much money *your money* has earned on an annualized basis.

If you invested $100,000 and received an annual distribution of $10,000, then you have a cash-on-cash return of 10% (Initial Investment / Return = CoC Return).

Most real estate investors seek around an 8% cash-on-cash return.

AVERAGE ANNUALIZED RETURN (AAR)

The average yearly historical return.

The average annualized return is one of the easier calculations to make. Simply divide your initial investment by your total profit, and then divide that number by how many years you held the investment.

This is a simple metric to calculate and understand, but we consider it inferior to the internal rate of return because it doesn't factor in the *timing* of when cash flows were received. Not accounting for the time value of money is a mistake in our book.

So, let's examine why that is by turning to the internal rate of return.

INTERNAL RATE OF RETURN (IRR)

The total time-adjusted returns of an investment.

The internal rate of return confuses most new investors. Heck, sometimes it even confuses experienced investors.

Here's the complicated definition: IRR is the *discount rate that makes the net present value (NPV) of all cash flows equal to zero.*

Did your eyes glaze over a bit? Yeah, mine too. So what's this mean in plain English?

Let's zoom out to the 50,000-foot view.

IRR measures the return of an investment by accounting for not only *what* was returned, but also *when* that *what* was returned. With the internal rate of return, time matters. Or, more precisely, *when you receive your money* matters.

So to calculate the internal rate of return, we start with our initial investment at time zero. From here, we tabulate cash flow distributions and any proceeds from capital events (refinance or sale). Then we bundle all those numbers together to produce one macro-return number that's adjusted for when you received those proceeds.

If this sounds complicated, that's because it is. To calculate this complex formula you'll need a spreadsheet with the IRR function. A pen and some paper won't cut it.

You might be asking yourself, why bother? Does it really matter all that much *when* we receive our money?

Absolutely it does.

Earlier we briefly mentioned the time value of money, the idea that a dollar in hand is worth more than two dollars in a bush (that's how you butcher an age-old saying, but you get the idea). There are two reasons for this.

1. **Inflation:** The value of a dollar generally lessens over time as more money is printed, thus increasing the supply. That, coupled with rising costs of living, means $1,000 next year (usually) buys less than $1,000 today.
2. **Utility:** Money is only as valuable as what you can do with it. Theoretical money is nice. Actual money is better.

Theoretical = Equity. Actual = Cash

Additionally, money in hand can be immediately reinvested. The more money you put to work, the more wealth you can accumulate.

So that's why $1 today is worth more than $1 next year. How much better? That's what the internal rate of return quantifies.

Let's consider two examples. We'll hold both projects for five years while executing completely different business models. Our total returns are identical. The only difference is *when* we receive our returns.

In example one, we have a development deal that produces zero cash flow throughout the life of the project. In year five, we'll receive one lump sum profit.

Example two is a classic value-add deal producing regular annual cash flow distributions coupled with a refinance in year two and sale in year five.

In both examples, the net returns are identical. You'll receive exactly the same amount of money in both scenarios, but we're going to tweak *when* you receive the money. All right, so let's see how this affects our internal rate of return, assuming an investment of $100,000.

In deal one, we invest $100,000 and receive zero cash flow distributions throughout the life of the investment. We sell the property in year five and receive $200,000, generating a $100,000 profit and a 14% IRR.

That's a solid return, but let's see what happens when we couple cash flow distributions with a refinance and sale.

Deal two delivers an 8% cash-on-cash return annually ($8,000/year). In year two, we execute a cash-out refinance and return 60% of your capital ($60,000). In year five, we sell the property and you receive another $108,000, bringing your total earnings to $100,000 (just like in the first deal).

Despite both projects producing identical total returns ($100,000), that second deal delivers a phenomenal IRR of *22%!*

That's an 8% higher return than in the first deal, gained simply by tweaking *when* we received distributions. None of the other commonly used return metrics accounts for the time value of money, which is what makes the IRR the gold standard of return metrics for us.

EQUITY MULTIPLE (EM)

The total amount of distributions received divided by the amount of initial investment.

This metric isn't terribly important, all things considered. It's a nice quick way to determine your projected net return on an investment. That's all.

Let's invest another $100,000 into a deal that will deliver a total return of $200,000 in five years. In this deal, we've doubled our money and achieved a 2x equity multiple. To calculate the equity multiple, simply divide total earnings ($200,000) by the initial investment amount

($100,000).

Not too shabby for a five-year hold.

Don't get too hung up on the equity multiple, though. It doesn't take into consideration the length of the deal, which makes it problematic. Presumably, longer projects lead to higher equity multiples. A deal delivering a 2.5x equity multiple over the course of ten years isn't necessarily better than a deal only delivering 2x over the span of five years.

The equity multiple does allow for a quick mental calculation of your total potential return. Beyond that, this metric shouldn't be used to justify funding one investment over another.

PREFERRED RETURN (PREF)

The claim on profits provided to investors.

That definition isn't terribly helpful. Let's clarify using an example from our typical deal structure at Invictus Capital.

We typically offer between a 6 and 8% preferred return to our limited partners, meaning our investors receive a 6–8% return on their investment before we (the deal sponsors) share in any of the returns. Once we've delivered that minimum return, the remainder of the profits above and beyond the preferred return are divided according to the equity split.

To use the jumbo jet analogy, the limited partners are guaranteed to receive dinner before the general partners get any food. If there's not enough chicken and salad to go around, then the general partners simply go hungry.

Preferred returns show that the deal sponsors have prioritized their investors by taking a backseat until they've provided a minimum satisfactory return on *your* money. These are great because they point to a better fiscal alignment of incentives between you and the deal sponsors.

Most often, the preferred return rolls over from year to year. If in any year the deal fails to deliver the full preferred return, then the remainder gets tacked onto following years until fully repaid. This is important where value-add deals are concerned. Often these projects don't achieve the full preferred return in the first year or two, when capital is being deployed to make renovations.

Without the rollover, any undelivered preferred return simply disappears at year-end—clearly not great for the passive investors. Be certain you know the nuances of how your operator plans to handle the preferred return before funding a deal.

Not all deals offer a preferred return, mind you. If you're considering investing in a deal without a preferred return, you should have an extra high degree of trust in the operator. Also, it never hurts to ask *why* the sponsor structured the deal in the way that they did. The answer to that question can impart some useful insight about the operator's principles.

CONCLUSION

There's an encyclopedia worth of return metrics out there in the universe. More information isn't necessarily a good thing, however. It's about being able to separate the signal from the noise.

If you understand these five metrics (cash-on-cash return, annualized average return, internal rate of return, equity multiple, and preferred return), then you'll be in a strong position to analyze any deal that comes across your desk.

CHAPTER 16

THE OPERATING STATEMENT

THE OPERATING STATEMENT

One of the first businesses I helped build was a climbing facility designed for young competitive athletes with grand aspirations of someday competing in national championships. My role was to develop the coaching program, maintain athlete relations, and bring in new business. This opportunity utilized my skill set as a former professional rock climber and a marketing fanatic. A match made in heaven, from my perspective.

Unfortunately, at that point in my career, I didn't have a clue how to read and understand a financial statement. I glossed over this weakness, assuming my partners had it covered. I trusted their diagnosis of the company's financial health. By the time I realized something was wrong, it was too late. We were dead in the water.

Too much money going out. Not enough coming in.

With only a couple months' worth of reserves left, we had some hard decisions to make. In a desperate last-ditch effort, we pivoted the business model and managed to extend the life of that business, but from that experience I learned an invaluable lesson: *you can't outsource reading the report card.*

Here's my confession. I hate spreadsheets.

Okay, that's not the weirdest confession ever. Unfortunately, when it comes to running a successful business, you can't avoid living in the spreadsheets at least a little.

I learned that lesson the hard way.

To help save you some of the heartache and headache I experienced, we're going to walk through a sample profit and loss statement highlighting the parts that you, the passive investor, need to know about.

Don't be like me. Don't let your fear of spreadsheets keep you from even looking at these reports. Even a passing understanding of what to look for (and where to look for it) can potentially save you, or a project, from absolute catastrophe.

Now, for those fresh off the boat, operating statements can come in all sorts of forms. In this chapter, we're specifically breaking these down into Income and Expense statements.

Let's take it from the top.

Income

Gross Potential Rent	$1,247,497	$1,284,922	$1,323,470
Loss to Lease	-$220,420	-$227,033	-$233,844
Bad Debt	-$14,783	-$15,226	-$15,683
Concessions	-$16,232	-$16,719	-$17,221
Vacancy	-$101,465	-$104,509	-$107,644
Net Rental Income	**$894,597**	**$921,435**	**$949,078**
Supplemental Income	$11,021	$11,352	$11,692
Utility Reimbursement	$36,785	$37,889	$39,025
Laundry Fee Income	$6,252	$6,440	$6,633
Parking Fee Income	$15,320	$15,780	$16,253
Storage Fee Income	$2,000	$2,060	$2,122
Pet Fee Income	$9,000	$9,270	$9,548
Effective Gross Income	**$974,975**	**$1,004,224**	**$1,034,351**

	Year 1	Year 2	Year 3
Expenses			
Property Taxes	147,697.00	150,650.94	153,663.96
Property and Liability Insurance	30,460.00	31,069.20	31,690.58
Utilities - Gas	32,071.00	32,712.42	33,366.67
Utiliteis - Electric	34,779.00	35,474.58	36,184.07
Utilities - Sewer & Water	71,299.00	72,724.98	74,179.48
Utilities - Trash Removal	19,272.00	19,657.44	20,050.59
Property Management	24,302.00	24,788.04	25,283.80
Payroll	18,823.00	19,199.46	19,583.45
Repairs and Maintenance	78,356.00	79,923.12	81,521.58
Contract Services	15,607.00	15,919.14	16,237.52
Turn Costs	23,049.00	23,509.98	23,980.18
Total Expenses	**$495,715.00**	**$505,629.30**	**$515,741.89**
Expense Ratio	51%	50%	50%
Net Operating Income	$ 479,260.00	$ 498,594.95	$ 518,609.09

INCOME

There's a lot of jargon when it comes to the income statement. You might hear this called a T-12 (trailing 12), T-3 (trailing 3), T-1 (trailing 1), or a whole slew of other names (APOD or Annual Property Operating Data).

From a quick high level, the T-whatevers are all effectively the same thing. They're a historical look-back on financial performance over a certain period of time. The number in the name designates the period of time.

The T-12, for instance, looks back at the trailing twelve months of performance, whereas the T-1 only looks at the previous month. The T-12 offers a more complete perspective of the property's performance over the course of a year and different seasons.

Unfortunately, sellers don't always have complete financial records, and we have to piece together whatever information we can to create our most reasonable forecasts. Sometimes all that's available is the previous month's performance.

Hey, nobody said this would be easy.

GROSS POTENTIAL RENT (GPR)

This is the ultimate performance watermark. If every unit rents at market rate and we collect the full amount each month, then the gross potential rent is how much the property will produce.

For example, fifty one-bedroom units that rent for the market rate of $1,000 per month produce an annualized gross potential rent of: 50 units x $1,000 rent x 12 months = $600,000.

So that's our absolute best-case scenario for rent collections. Mind you, it's not really an achievable number. It's simply the benchmark.

LOSS-TO-LEASE (LTL)

The loss-to-lease is any amount we fail to collect of the GPR.

Again, using the previous example, if market rent for our fifty units is $1,000 but we only collect $975 on average, then our loss-to-lease is: $600,000 GPR – 50 units x $975 average rent x 12 months = $15,000 LTL.

The LTL tells us at a glance how efficiently the property is operating. On a long enough horizon (two to four years), you should see this number floating between 1 and 3%.

BAD DEBT

Got tenants who failed to pay rent, late fees, parking, or any other such fee? At a certain point, you write that money off and assume it's gone forever. We call this bad debt.

Sometimes this number can be found in the expense category, but we personally deduct it straight from the GPR.

What's an acceptable amount of bad debt?

That depends on the property class, location, tenant base, and business plan. This number could skyrocket past 3% on an asset where the value-add revolves around replacing bad tenants with good tenants. Then again, on a stabilized asset with a great tenant base, this number shouldn't be much higher than 0.5%.

CONCESSIONS

Sometimes when you're in a hot market with lots of competition, would-be tenants need a little something extra to sweeten the pot, like a free first month's rent. Concessions are entirely market and asset class dependent.

In our market (Minneapolis and St. Paul), we rarely ever see concessions offered on Class C and B assets. Newer buildings, on the other hand, frequently offer discounted first month rents or other move-in bonuses to entice new tenants.

Whatever concessions are made, that number cuts into the gross potential rent.

VACANCY

There are two types of vacancy: physical and economic.

Physical vacancy is straightforward. It's how many units are rented versus how many units there are total. If we have one hundred total units and ninety-eight are currently leased, then we are 2% vacant. The inverse of that statement is that we're 98% occupied.

The dollar amount of loss and percentage of total loss are expressed on the operating statement and offer quick, valuable insight into the property's operations.

Economic vacancy is, practically speaking, the more important metric of the two. It tells us how much we're *actually* collecting in rent versus gross potential rent.

To calculate economic vacancy, we add up all the things that have reduced our GPR (loss-to-lease, bad debt, concessions, etc.). This number is expressed as a percentage and can be quite high in the early years of a value-add project. Many operating statements will not explicitly list out this number, so you might have to calculate it yourself.

This number is critical to know in relation to another important concept called the **break-even occupancy**. The break-even occupancy is the number below which the property is no longer able to sustain the debt service. If you're not well-enough capitalized and you fall below this number, the project is in dire straights.

This number can be an effective way to gauge a project's potential risk. Ask your operator about this number and then weigh the probability of the project ever treading in waters too close to that death zone.

We look for break-even occupancy numbers around 70% for the types of projects we pursue. This is a healthy margin of safety in our eyes. For one of our projects to balloon up to 30% economic vacancy, something will have to have gone horrifically wrong.

Then again, a heavy value-add project might easily eclipse this number. There is no right or wrong rule of thumb. The variables must be weighed against the project's unique context.

NET RENTAL INCOME (NRI)

Net rental income is simply the *actual* amount of rent received. To calculate this number, take your gross potential rent and subtract from it loss-to-lease, bad debt, concessions, and vacancy.

SUPPLEMENTAL INCOME

Rent accounts for the majority of revenue generated by a multifamily asset, but it's not all the revenue. New operators often get tunnel vision looking at ways to increase rent when there are, in fact, a number of other ways to add tremendous value to an asset's net operating income.

Savvy operators realize that sometimes the majority of value to be added to a property comes by way of supplemental income.

In addition to pet rents, other great sources of supplemental income include coin-operated laundry, paid storage, and paid parking spaces (or garage access, if available). Remember, given the multiplying effect of dividing our NOI by the cap rate, small increases in revenue (even a few cents on laundry, for example) go a long way toward improving a building's valuation.

Another income source you'll often find (and sometimes this will appear broken out onto a separate line on the operating statement) is RUBS (Ratio Utility Billback System).

EFFECTIVE GROSS INCOME

If gross potential rent is our pie-in-the-sky, absolute best-case scenario for rent collection, then effective gross income is our boots-in-the-mud *actual* collected revenue after we add up all collected rent plus supplemental income.

Sometimes the difference between the GPR and EGI can be quite large, depending on the efficiency of operations.

EXPENSES

You know how I feel about the value of saving a dollar versus earning a new one. Remember, a dollar saved is worth more than a dollar earned.

With that said, cutting expenses is much easier said than done. Many a new operator has thought they could run a property more efficiently than the mom-and-pop team who've been running it for the past thirty years, only to find out implementing operational improvements is harder than anticipated.

Some of these operators burn out. Others adapt and overcome.

All the potential expenses of a property are represented on this next section of the operating statement. Here are the expense levers your worthy operator might pull to extract maximum value from an asset.

TAXES

Property taxes are pretty straightforward and obvious, right?

Well, you'd think so. Surprisingly, one of the most common mistakes new investors make is to project future tax bills based on the seller's current tax appraisal.

This is a glaring oversight. You can be certain that after you acquire a property, the city, county, or whoever is going to come by for a new assessment, and that number is going to be based off what you *just* paid, and not whatever the seller paid for it when they purchased the property.

If the seller has owned the property for more than a couple years, then the difference between those two numbers can be staggering.

There is no one universal way to calculate property tax. This will vary area by area. One of the most common methods multiplies the property's assessed value by a mill rate.

Passive investors don't need to get too in the weeds on this. You're merely looking to see that the sponsor has appropriately accounted for an increasing tax bill in year one or two.

INSURANCE

Nobody enjoys paying their monthly insurance premium, but it sure comes in handy if somebody drives a car through the building's lobby. This is an extreme example, but it happens far more often than you might imagine. For whatever reason, multifamily assets are a lightning rod for situations where insurance is indispensable. This is one of those areas where you definitely don't want to skimp.

Whether it's protecting against fire, flood, or simple liability claims, you need to cover your bases. It's not a matter *if* something will go wrong. It's simply a matter of *when*.

Now, insurance prices vary based on a multitude of factors. A property at higher risk of natural disaster (say, in New Orleans) will have a drastically different premium than an asset in the middle of Wyoming.

It's reasonable to assume that insurance costs will be slightly higher than what's currently in place. How much higher is impossible to say.

Ask your operator for a detailed breakdown of their insurance coverage plus the highest risk factors they anticipate covering against.

UTILITIES

Utilities are one of the largest ongoing expenses a property will incur. Anything we can do to increase efficiency pays massive dividends.

One fantastic way of reducing utilities is by billing back a portion of the water, gas, or electricity expenses to the tenant. Unfortunately, this only goes so far. There are a number of common-area utilities you'll have to pay. Because of the size and scale of these apartment communities, making energy-saving improvements is often well worth the time and expense.

These improvements may include LED lighting or low-flow toilets, faucets, and shower heads. A little can go a long way here.

Sometimes you'll find individual utilities (electricity, common-area electricity, water, gas/sewer) broken out individually on the operating statement. Sometimes it will all be lumped into one single bucket. That can make it difficult to determine where exactly all the numbers are coming from.

For instance, does that number include trash collection or does that fall under contract services? There's no right or wrong answer, but it's helpful to know how your sponsor is accounting for these details in the operating statement.

PROPERTY MANAGEMENT

This expense line covers the cost of property management and should be calculated as a percentage of effective gross income. This means the management company's compensation is tied to the amount of revenue generated by the property on a month-by-month basis, which is what you want. Calculating their fee in any other way is problematic.

Most operators outsource property management to a professional third-party company. Management fees vary from 2 to 10% depending on asset class and size. The larger the property, the lower the percentage. A 200-unit complex, for example, might only have a 2% management fee, whereas a single-family home might be closer to 10%.

All told, these fees might not seem so bad. Unfortunately, they're not the full picture.

PAYROLL

Large properties command less of a fee because they require on-site staff. The rule of thumb is that two staff persons are required for every one hundred units: one in the office and one working maintenance.

The payroll line-item accounts for their salaries and any other costs associated with their employment.

Once we factor this number alongside the property management fee, the effective expense ratio crawls up closer to 10% of the effective gross income.

If, on the other hand, your operator has built an in-house property management team, they'll typically be able to operate the property (with the same amount of staff) for closer to 4–5% of EGI.

From the beginning, we built Invictus Capital with an in-house property management team for two reasons:

1) We love serving our residents directly and knowing that we're in full control over our investments.

2) We're instantly 5% more competitive on our offers than our competitors who rely on third-party management.

There is no right or wrong here. Just different strokes for different folks.

REPAIRS AND MAINTENANCE

This category can be a real hot mess when digging through the financial records of mom-and-pop owners. Many of these operators fail to correctly distinguish between repairs and capital expenditures.

The quick rule of thumb is that a capital expenditure (CapEx) item adds to the useful life of the property, whereas a repair merely returns a thing to operational status.

Why does this matter?

Because these expenses appear on completely different sections of the operating statement or profit and loss statement (P&L). Repairs and maintenance are considered operational expenses, so they appear above the line (NOI), whereas CapEx items are capital improvements and fall below the line.

That might not mean much to you, but here's the important takeaway: When CapEx items land in the repairs and maintenance bucket, it makes the property appear as though it's required more repairs than it actually does. On the flip side, if repairs and maintenance find their way into the CapEx bucket, then the property will appear to require less in these areas than is accurate. Both situations are problematic for completely different reasons.

So what exactly qualifies as repair and maintenance? Anything necessary for the continued operation of the property. This includes the materials and labor involved in a plumber servicing a clogged pipe or an HVAC service-person tuning the furnace.

It's difficult to peg per-unit repair averages to a rule of thumb number. So much depends on asset age, class, and the business model being deployed. Rather than looking for a specific number, it's more important to understand the *story* behind the number. This'll require asking some questions of your operator to decide for yourself if the amount allocated for repairs and maintenance makes sense.

CONTRACT SERVICES

Any recurring monthly (or annual) service falls into the category of contract services.

The most common contract services are trash collection, landscaping, laundry, snow removal, pool services, and pest control. Shouldn't some of these expenses fall under repairs and maintenance?

Not if there's a signed contract with the expectation of ongoing service. If it's a one-time fix, it's a repair. If the contractor comes back every month, it's a contract service.

That's pretty straightforward, right?

TURN COSTS

Functionally no different than repairs and maintenance, these expenses are incurred as a result of turning a unit after one tenant moves out and before the next moves in. This includes both material costs and labor.

The thing to note here is that these improvements are the small cosmetic improvements required to *clean-up* between tenants. This doesn't include CapEx improvements to add new appliances, flooring, fixtures, etc. Because these costs improve the functional life of the property, they are not considered operational expenses and are accounted for differently.

Don't be surprised if your operator doesn't break out this line item. Many operators simply attribute turn costs to repairs and maintenance. We find it's helpful to distinguish the two, because bucketing them together can muddle the waters of how efficiently the asset is being maintained.

TOTAL EXPENSES AND EXPENSE RATIO

Once we bucket all of our expenses together, we're going to land on a macro-operating expense number. This number is critical in determining the overall operational efficiency of the building.

We determine that efficiency by dividing our operating expenses by our effective gross income. The resulting number gives us our expense ratio—that is, what percentage of our revenue goes toward expenses.

This number is vital. If we know the expense ratio of comparable assets in an area, then we can know at a glance how efficiently the property in question is being run.

A good starting point is a 50% expense ratio. That means, for every dollar that comes in, fifty cents go toward expenses. Great operators will have an expense ratio in the low 40s, whereas poor operators will float up into the 60s.

Be aware of an operator's projections if their business plan anticipates operating a property below a 40% expense ratio. It's possible, but a whole lot of efficiencies have to be realized in order to hit those types of numbers consistently.

An expense ratio around 45% on a stabilized asset is a conservative number that most competent operators can hit.

NET OPERATING INCOME

Now we arrive at the most important number of them all: net operating income.

If you weren't sleep-reading through the earlier chapters on how multi-family assets are valued, then you fully understand why this number is so critical.

After accounting for all our income and expenses, we can calculate this all-important number with confidence.

Remember, we calculate net operating income before accounting for debt service and CapEx. This is because investors need an apples-to-apples way of comparing potential properties. Debt service depends on multiple factors that can skew these comparisons, factors ranging from an operator's strength as a borrower, the status of the property at the time of the loan, the macro-lending environment, and the particular bank or resource utilized in the initial financing.

Simply put, these variables fluctuate too widely to be helpful in calculating a property's value.

So we strip those out and look purely at the amount of income an asset produces minus the expenses required to keep it operational. The result is our net operating income.

PROJECTIONS

"It's ain't what you don't know that gets you into trouble. It's what you know for sure that just ain't so."

— Mark Twain

no deal sponsor will tell you with a straight face that they know what the future holds. And yet, in the business of investing, we must make predictions about what we think the future will bring.

Assumptions are unavoidable. One way or another, you're banking on the future being either better or worse than the present. Successful investors aren't necessarily the ones who predict correctly, they're the ones who position themselves to succeed regardless of 99% of potential outcomes.

Nassim Taleb calls this the barbell strategy, where we stand to gain disproportionately in relation to losses. Asymmetric returns, baby.

Of course, this is all much easier said than done.

So how do we do it? How do we position ourselves to succeed regardless of what the market does in the future?

Well, step one is to simply assume the worst. If your numbers still work, huzzah! If you're wrong about the future and it turns out better than expected, then you only stand to outperform.

Granted, an absolute worst-case scenario would be some combination of events ending in pure Armageddon-style catastrophe. It's unlikely your investment strategy will continue to work if an asteroid plays a game of galactic pool with planet Earth.

So how are we to reasonably predict a *survivable worst-case scenario*?

This is where sensitivity testing comes in.

In a sensitivity test, we push and pull on a number of variables to see where the project survives and where it falls apart. Then, once we have a spectrum of potential scenarios, we map those against historical data to see how the property would have performed during the last great market downturn. At the time of this writing, that means we look to the 2008 financial crisis.

Sensitivity testing helps paint a picture, but don't fall in love with u..
results. We must never forget that if we had utilized this same strategy
in 2007, months before the financial market imploded, our models would
have proved insufficient.

That's because we would've been benchmarking off the *then* worst-case
scenario. The *next* worst-case scenario we experience will be worse than
any scenario that's ever come before. That's the nature of worst-case
scenarios. They keep getting worse.

The important takeaway here is not to throw our hands up in despair
or completely sit out of the market because we have no way of safely
predicting the future. Those two strategies (despair and inaction) are
guaranteed ways to lose out. In the end, we must accept that investing is
inherently risky and hedge against the unknown by deploying reasonably
conservative assumptions in our underwriting.

Here are three assumptions you want to pay close attention to in particular
when it comes to projecting future performance:

1. Rent growth
2. Expense growth
3. Cap rate

These are the three most important levers when it comes to increasing our
property's value. It behooves us to err on the side of caution when making
projections based on these numbers. If we're even slightly overly optimistic in our cap rate projections, for instance, it can skew our expected
returns by orders of magnitude.

Here are a couple rules to keep in mind when evaluating these metrics.

First, assume expenses will increase. It's unlikely the price of labor, utilities, or supplies will drop. A healthy market typically inflates, which means
that despite your best operational efforts, your expenses will increase

every year. 2–3% is a healthy assumption that trends closely with the rate of inflation over the past decade.

Second, we must employ pessimism when predicting how rent growth and cap rates will fluctuate in the future.

Simply put, assume the metrics that can help us (rent and cap rate) will perform poorly while the metrics that can hurt us (expenses) will grow.

Rent growth is market-dependent. Some areas have experienced incredible organic rent appreciation over the past decade. Past performance is no guarantee of future performance, however. We have no rule of thumb to offer you here in terms of what to look for. Question your operator's assumptions, how those assumptions jive with past performance, and what potential future events could derail those expectations.

If they can't answer any of those questions, then you'd best be walking to the door.

Cap rates, again, are market dependent. Because this metric is so disproportionately impactful, we suggest assuming the cap rate will soften by at least ten basis points per year over the life of a project. So if you purchased at a 6% cap rate today, then in five years you could reasonably assume it'll be around 6.5%.

Remember, cap rates are inversely proportional to the value, so the bigger the percentage, the less our building are worth.

In all things pertaining to investing and the future, our advice is to underwrite with extreme pessimism.

AND KNOWING IS HALF THE BATTLE

Listen, I get it. Spreadsheets and numbers makes my eyes glaze over, too. Unfortunately, when it comes to investing, the numbers are everything.

It's not enough to have a great idea or to project incredible returns. You have to execute a plan capable of delivering those returns.

The operating statement is vital to your understanding of whether the deal sponsor is being realistic in their return projections. Now that you're aware of all the individual parts comprising a property's income and expenses, you're armed to ask better questions and to make better decisions.

With that said, there's still one more piece of the multifamily engine that you *must* understand: *the debt.*

CHAPTER 17

UNDERSTANDING THE DEBT

UNDERSTANDING THE DEBT

Leverage is a large part of what makes real estate such a powerful investment vehicle.

Bank financing enables investors to acquire cash-flow-generating multifamily assets for only a fraction of a property's value. If you've purchased a home, chances are you didn't pay for it with straight cash. Most people utilize bank financing in the form of a mortgage, requiring them to come to the closing table with a down payment of only around 20% of the home's value.

Debt gets a bad name because people fail to distinguish between good debt and bad debt. Most people simply don't know the difference.

Bad debt is consumer debt used to purchase liabilities. What's a liability? Anything that takes money out of your pocket. Most Americans carry significant credit card debt that they've used to purchase clothes, food, travel, and entertainment.

Good debt, on the other hand, is used to purchase assets. Assets, like a cash-flow-producing property, put cash back *in* your pocket.

When viewed through this lens, many of the things most people consider assets (your personal residence and car, for example) are, in fact, simply liabilities.

We're not suggesting you pay all cash for your primary residence or that you should eschew owning a home and simply rent. Depending on your life circumstances, there could be many great reasons for using debt to facilitate these purchases. The key is recognizing the difference between the type of debt that goes toward *consumption* and the type of debt utilized in acquiring *income-generating* assets.

If you've been raised to view debt as risky, then these few short paragraphs are unlikely to change your mind. That's okay. Familiarity breeds confidence.

Through the rest of this chapter we're going to talk in detail about the different components of the debt structure utilized in purchasing multi-family assets.

Before we get to that, let's talk about who we're actually getting the money from.

AGENCY VERSUS PORTFOLIO

In the world of multifamily real estate, most loans are originated either through one of two government-backed agencies (Fannie May and Freddie Mac) or through a portfolio lender (community bank or credit union).

Agency debt is a government-backed mortgage and offers the best options when seeking long-term, secure financing with favorable terms. It's usually hard to beat agency debt when it comes to interest rates and term periods. If you have a stabilized asset you're planning to hold for a long time, you'd be hard-pressed to do better than an agency loan.

So, what's the downside?

For starters, these loans are notoriously difficult to qualify for. These government-backed loans are only available to borrowers with strong track records coupled with strong personal financial statements. Most notably, the deal sponsors must possess a certain liquidity *and* have a net worth equal to (and sometimes even larger than) the loan amount.

This creates a high hurdle when acquiring properties worth tens of millions of dollars.

Additionally, agency loans are only available for stabilized properties achieving certain performance metrics. This works great for yield plays on Class A properties, but not so much on value-add deals where we specifically seek to find underperforming assets with unrealized potential.

Another nail in the coffin for value-add deals is the fact that agency loans often come with a hefty prepayment penalty (something we'll discuss later in this chapter).

These downsides lead most operators specializing in value-add opportunities to utilize a bridge loan during the repositioning phase of a deal with the plan of refinancing into agency debt once the property is stabilized.

A portfolio lender, by comparison to the agency alternative, is an entity (community bank or credit union, for example) who keeps the loan on their own books. Since they don't sell it to a government agency, they're able to dictate their own terms.

Community banks and credit unions are great because you can work with them one-on-one to explain the nuances of the deal to create win-win terms for all sides. Forging strong professional relationships with local lenders is critical.

This is an often-overlooked value of a great operator: their network of relationships. Don't underestimate the power of a great network when you're considering partnering with a sponsorship team.

Usually, the trade-off of a bridge loan is that the terms are less competitive than through an agency. Expect higher interest rates, shorter terms, shorter interest-only periods, and less amortization, not to mention a prepayment penalty.

There is no one-size-fits-all solution when it comes to choice of lender. Pairing the right deal with the right debt sometimes means working with Fannie and Freddie, while other times it means staying local.

These are all tools in a toolbox. It's your operator's job to know when to reach for the screwdriver rather than the hammer.

The passive investor's goal is to understand enough that when the deal sponsor holds up a prospective tool, they can at least tell whether it'll get the job done. To that end, let's talk about the parts that comprise these various tools.

Anticipated Senior Debt

Loan Type	Bank Debt
Term	5 Years
Months of IO	24
Fixed/Adjustable	Fixed
Amortization	25 Years
Pre-Payment	3,2,1
Loan Amount	$ 2,812,500.00
Interest Rate	3.75%
Loan to Value	75%

Example of Debt Structure from an Actual Invictus Capital Deal

INTEREST

Most people are familiar with the concept of interest rates. Interest is the rate of return the bank expects to receive as a percentage of the amount loaned. Broadly speaking, lower interest rates are better than higher interest rates when borrowing.

If a bank loans you $100,000 at 10% interest, then they'll annually receive $10,000. That's fairly straightforward.

Here's something a little trickier. Sometimes the interest rate is fixed and sometimes it's adjustable. A fixed-rate interest loan is exactly what it sounds like. The interest rate is locked in when the loan is originated and never changes. An adjustable-rate mortgage (ARM), by comparison, *does* fluctuate over time, usually in relation to some stated standard (London Inter-bank Offered Rate (LIBOR) or Secured Overnight Financing Rate (SOFR), depending on when you're reading this).

TERM

A loan's term is how long you have to pay back the debt.

The most common residential mortgage terms for a primary residence are fifteen and thirty years. Terms on commercial loans are quite a bit shorter, often ranging between five and ten years.

How much of the loan is paid off by the end of the term depends on the *amortization period*, which we'll discuss next, but it's helpful to point out that very little of a commercial loan's principal is actually paid off by the end of its term. This means a *balloon payment* is required when the terms ends. A balloon payment is a one-time payment for the remainder of a loan.

This is a double-edged blade. We prefer long terms (ten years or more) that provide plenty of runway to weather different market cycles and select the opportune moments to either refinance or sell. Unfortunately, sometimes it's necessary to take out a bridge loan with a shorter term (three years, for example) while repositioning a property.

The shorter the term, the less you can afford for things to go wrong in your budget, reposition, or market cycle.

Never go into a deal until you know how you're getting out. Start with the end in mind and pay close attention to where you are in the market cycle.

The importance of the term is often overlooked when evaluating bank debt. That's a mistake. If the bank note comes due at the wrong moment in the market's cycle, you might find yourself in the unenviable position of being a **motivated seller**.

AMORTIZATION PERIOD

If "term" is one of the simpler concepts to understand, "amortization period" might be one of the trickiest.

The **amortization period** is the time frame over which regular payments of interest and principal are sufficient to repay the loan in its entirety by the note's maturity date.

I know, that definition isn't super helpful. Let's use an example.

Often the amortization period and term on a residential loan used for buying a home are identical. If we have a thirty-year term and amortization, that means we have thirty years to pay off the loan and that each individual payment will be calculated by dividing the loan balance into 360 equal payments.

Wait, where did the 360 come from?

Unless you have some strange arrangement with your bank, you're not making one single mortgage payment every year. Instead, you're paying monthly. Therefore, the payments are calculated as 12 months x 30 years = 360 payments.

And that's amortization.

But wait, what happens when the amortization period and term length *aren't* the same (as is often the case with commercial real estate)?

New investors are often confused by the fact that the amortization period and term length are rarely the same on a commercial loan. For instance, the term might be ten years with a thirty-year amortization period. Doing the math on that, we find we've only made 120 mortgage payments (10 years x 12 months = 120 payments) by the end of the term when the loan comes due.

This is where the balloon payment comes into play.

Most operations don't keep enough cash handy to cover such a payment, so one of two things typically occurs well before the balloon payment comes due:

1. The property is refinanced
2. The property is sold

Amortization is an important lever impacting the monthly debt service. A longer amortization period is often better from an investment perspective because it spreads payments out over a longer period, thus reducing your single largest monthly expense: the mortgage. Commercial loans typically have amortization periods between twenty and twenty-five years.

INTEREST-ONLY (IO)

Learning about interest-only periods for the first time blew my mind. It was a proverbial light-bulb moment that put into perspective how eager banks are to lend on cash-flow-generating commercial real estate.

An interest-only period is pretty straightforward. During this period (usually between one and five years), you only make interest payments on the mortgage. Once the IO period expires, the monthly debt service will now include both principal and interest payments.

Interest-only periods are an incredible resource that reduces monthly debt service during a project's early years, when capital expenditures are high and cash flow is tight. Most value-add deals are, by definition, not operating at their full potential from day one. They might have high vacancy, below-market rents, or significant deferred maintenance. These improvements take time.

The interest-only period helps buy the project that needed time.

Now, one big risk associated with an interest-only period is that it can make a deal look a whole lot better than it really is in the first couple years. It's like a Band-Aid for a questionable investment. Eventually it has to come off, and when it does, you might not care for what you see underneath.

Pay particularly close attention to what happens to cash flow in the years after the interest-only period expires.

The operator's game plan might be to refinance into long-term debt in years two or three, thus reducing the importance of what happens after the interest-only period ends, but it never hurts to ask: **What happens if the market gets wobbly between now and that hypothetical refinance? What if the business plan is falling behind schedule and a refinance isn't feasible?**

These are important questions to consider *before* funding a deal.

LOAN-TO-VALUE (LTV)

The loan-to-value tells us how leveraged a property is relative to its underlying value. If you have a mortgage for $800,000 on a building worth

$1,000,000, then the LTV (loan-to-value) is 80%.

Most banks will loan between 65 and 80% of a commercial property's value. This leaves you, the borrower, to bring the remaining 20–35% to the closing table in the form of a down payment.

That's not an inconsequential amount of money when acquiring buildings worth millions of dollars. This is where syndications come into play.

Loan-to-value is tricky and it's not always clear how much debt you should put on a property. An investor seeking to maximize their cash-on-cash return might want a higher LTV (say 80%). There are, however, downstream consequences to this strategy.

Putting less money into a deal theoretically boosts returns, but at the expense of an increased monthly debt service, which thins out cash flow. As cash flow diminishes, so too does the property's ability to absorb unexpected operational difficulties.

So there are pros and cons to both sides of the LTV coin. Which is right for any particular deal depends largely on market cycle, business plan, and operational prowess. In the end it'll largely come down to your risk tolerance coupled with your desired outcome.

We tend toward a conservative approach that maintains an LTV around 65–75%.

LOAN-TO-COST (LTC)

The little brother to LTV, loan-to-cost (LTC) is a metric used most often when there's a construction component to a project, which is often the case in a value-add deal. With loan-to-cost, the lender allows you to wrap the cost of construction into the initial loan, which can then be utilized for renovations and other CapEx.

DEBT SERVICE COVERAGE RATIO (DSCR)

The debt service coverage ratio (DSCR) is one of the most important metrics a bank considers when underwriting a property. The DSCR is the ratio between an asset's net operating income and total debt service (DSCR = NOI / Debt Service).

That is, it tells you how much than just the debt service an asset is generating in revenue.

If a property earns $120,000 in yearly NOI with a debt service of $100,000, then the DSCR is 1.2 ($120,000 / $100,000). A DSCR greater than 1.0 means the property generates more cash than it pays out in debt. Below 1.0 and you're officially in the red and more funds will be required (from somewhere) to cover the debt service.

It doesn't take a financial wizard to figure out that you won't survive long with a DSCR below 1.0. In fact, most lenders require a DSCR of at least 1.20. In their eyes, this indicates an asset with sufficient cash flow to weather operational issues regardless of market volatility.

RECOURSE VERSUS NON-RECOURSE

One of the beautiful things about passive investing in apartment syndications is that the limited partners don't personally guarantee the bank loan. If the project goes sideways for whatever reason, the bank can't go after you personally. This is where the *limited* part of the title comes in.

Limited activity. Limited risk.

The bank has no recourse against you, the passive investor. The risk you run in an apartment syndication is limited to the possibility of losing your initial investment.

The deal sponsors don't get the same protections. One of the critical roles filled by the deal sponsors is that of loan guarantor.

In the case of a recourse loan, this means they are personally guaranteeing the loan so that, in the case of a default, the bank can go after both the property itself and the sponsor's personal assets.

The alternative is a non-recourse loan, which is only backed by the property itself. Theoretically, in this scenario, the sponsors would have limited liability (like the passive investors). In reality, there are certain clauses and exceptions (e.g. bad boy carveouts) whereby the bank can go after an operator's assets in cases where the sponsor acted in bad faith or through incompetence.

No matter how you slice it, the sponsors carry quite a lot more risk than the limited partners.

CASH-OUT REFINANCE

This is the most powerful weapon in the value-add operator's arsenal. I struggled conceptually with the cash-out refinance when I first started investing. Part of it just seemed too good to be true.

To understand the cash-out refinance, let's return to the basics of value-add multifamily.

Remember, multifamily properties are valued like a business. The more profit they generate, the more they're worth. The most important number within our control is the net operating income (NOI) which is calculated by subtracting operational expenses (excluding debt service) from total revenue. When we divide that NOI by the market's capitalization rate, we get the building's fair-market value.

The value-add part comes in when we make upgrades to the property that lead to either increasing rents or decreasing expenses.

Let's say we acquired a hundred-unit apartment community with an average rent of $500 (yearly revenue = $600,000) and a 50% operational expense margin, leaving us with an NOI of $300,000. Assuming a 7% cap rate, our building at the time of purchase is worth $4,285,714.

If, after a year of renovations, upgrades, and improvements, we've increased the average rent by $100/unit to $600 total (yearly revenue = $720,000), and our operational expenses ratio remains at 50%, then our new NOI is $360,000. Dividing this new NOI by the cap rate of 7% indicates our building is now worth $5,142,857.

We've added $850,000+ of value in only one year. Unfortunately, this is only theoretical value until we have money in hand. At the moment, all our value is tied up in the form of equity.

This is where the cash-out refinance comes in.

We take out a new loan on the property at the new *higher* valuation, use a portion of that to pay off the old loan, and then pocket the difference.

Returning to our previous example, if we take out a 75% LTV loan on $5,142,857 (or $5,100,000, for simplicity's sake), our new loan amount is $3,825,000. If we'd taken out a similar 75% LTV loan when we'd originally purchased the property for $4,285,714 (or $4,200,000 for simplicity), then our original bank note is $3,150,000.

The majority of our new loan ($3,825,000) goes toward paying off the balance of the old loan ($3,150,000). The remaining $675,000 is deposited right back into our bank accounts.

These returns could be handled in a couple different ways. Most commonly, this money flows back to the passive investors to repay their original investment. Investors love the cash-out refinance because it's a non-taxable event that reduces the amount of money they have locked up in a deal.

Imagine walking into a casino and betting $100 on a single hand of blackjack. If you win, you're now $100 richer and can put your original $100 back in your pocket and continue playing entirely with house money.

This is effectively what happens in a cash-out refinance.

Something to pay particularly close to attention to in the operating agreement (which we'll cover in more depth in a coming chapter) is whether the return of capital dilutes your ownership. The majority of deals are structured such that the returned capital does *not* change your percentage ownership in the deal. In some opportunities, however, that's not the case. These deals are structured so that your ownership basis is reduced in relation to the amount of money returned.

In these deals, you are effectively *bought out.*

Obviously this is great for the sponsors who end up owning more (if not all) of the deal. It's less great for the limited partners, who don't get to participate in a potentially lucrative disposition.

We're not issuing any broad-reaching condemnations. There are some good reasons why an operator might structure an opportunity in this way. If they're presenting it honestly and clearly from the beginning and you're investing with full visibility, then there's nothing wrong with this structure.

PREPAYMENT PENALTY

The cash-out refinance is an amazing resource when properly executed, but it's not a silver bullet. There are certain occasions when a refinance is not ideal. Often this revolves around the prepayment penalty.

A prepayment penalty is a fee incurred for paying off a loan prematurely.

At first glance that might seem unfair, but let's look at it from the bank's perspective. A bank doesn't want to go through all the hassle of underwriting and originating a loan if they only stand to gain a tiny fraction of the expected return because you refinanced within the first twelve to twenty-four months.

Many community banks and portfolio lenders understand the value-add business model and the desire for a quick refinance. The trade-off comes in the form of higher interest rates or shorter terms.

Prepayment penalties come in a couple different varieties. The two most common in commercial real estate are **yield maintenance** and **step-down**.

Yield maintenance allows the lender to obtain the same total return, as though the borrower had kept the loan through maturation. If you have a ten-year term and refinance in year two, the yield maintenance is for the amount of total interest that *would have* accrued had the loan been held for the duration of the term. This form of prepayment penalty can suck all the juice out of an otherwise great deal.

The step-down method is a bit less painful. In this structure, the fee for exiting the loan early decreases every year until eventually disappearing altogether. A common structure might have a fee of 5% in year one, 4% in year two, 3% in year three, 2% in year four, and 1% in year five. If you can't secure a loan without a prepayment penalty, the step-down approach is typically your next best option.

It's important that your operator accounts for the potential impact of a prepayment penalty if a refinance or early sale is planned. The fees can quickly ruin return projections.

Oftentimes the prepayment penalty can be skirted by having a strong relationship with a local lender and by agreeing to refinance the loan through them. They're generally agreeable to this arrangement if you originate the new loan with them.

CAPITAL RESERVES

Depending on the loan provider and the current state of the market, you'll need to bring enough money to closing to cover the down payment, closing costs, capital expenditures, and capital reserves.

How much the bank requires varies. Often it's around six months' worth of principal and interest that goes into escrow until the project clears certain hurdles.

Take note that these requirements can change capriciously and in the blink of an eye. During the early months of the COVID pandemic in 2020, banks changed their requirements overnight. Suddenly, many operators with deals in progress found the bank requiring a full twelve months' worth of principal and interest in reserve. Needless to say, that's enough to nuke most people's underwriting.

Reserves are somewhat annoying when times are good and your money just sits dead in a bank. Then again, nobody's ever complained about having too much in reserve when times turn less good (or downright bad).

Capital reserves aren't something passive investors need to know much about. We simply mention them here to provide a complete view of all the interlocking pieces of the lending puzzle.

Listen, there's a lot to know when it comes to taking on debt. And I know this section wasn't the most riveting. Few people thoroughly enjoy digging into loan terms.

But the successful execution of an apartment syndication relies upon pairing the right debt with the right deal. The bank is your most important partner. In the same way you thoroughly vetted the deal sponsor, it's important you do the same with your debt partner.

PART SIX

THE PROCESS

CHAPTER 18

THE STEP-BY-STEP PROCESS

"You have to put in the time, but more important is the judgment. The direction you're heading in matters more than how fast you drive."

— Naval Ravikant

GOING UNDER CONTRACT

New real estate investors are often told that, for every one hundred deals they underwrite, about twenty will warrant a physical tour, ten justify submitting offers, and one will ultimately make it to closing.

In our experience, these numbers aren't too far off the mark. All told, a lot of work goes into getting a property under contract—a lot of work that you, the passive investor, thankfully don't have to do.

Although you don't have to do the work, it's helpful knowing what exactly goes into locking down a property, if for no other reason than so that you can gain a better appreciation for what the operators you've chosen to partner with are doing on your behalf.

TOURS

It's rare to put a property under contract sight unseen. Depending on your relationship with the seller or your familiarity with an area, it's possible, though not recommended. Putting boots on the ground for an initial walk-through with the broker or seller to view a couple units and sneak a peek at the mechanicals is advised before submitting an offer.

This initial tour is by no means exhaustive. At this point, your partners are simply looking for a high-level understanding of the property's potential upside and downside. With this information they'll dial in their underwriting and submit a letter of intent.

LETTER OF INTENT AND PURCHASE AND SALES AGREEMENT (LOI AND PSA)

First, the letter of intent (LOI) is not a legally binding contract.

Second, it's a bit of a formality that will sometimes be skipped entirely.

The LOI outlines the broad strokes of the buyer's offer. It typically includes a proposed purchase price, amount of earnest money, length of physical and financial due diligence, suggested closing date, and general information about the buyer.

Depending on the relationship with the seller, the LOI could be little more than scribbles on the back of a napkin. At other times, it's a couple-page document that kind of resembles a contract, except nobody actually signs the thing.

The seller will weed through the LOIs of prospective buyers to arrive at the top two or three offers. From there, we go to the Best and Final Round, a glorified way of pitting buyers against one another in a bidding war. This is one of the great advantages of finding deals off market: no competition.

If the seller awards your partners the contract, the deal then moves to the Purchase and Sale Agreement (PSA), which is a more detailed version of the letter of intent.

The important thing about the PSA is that it *is* a contract. As such, there will typically be some back-and-forth between the buyer's lawyers and the seller's lawyers to hammer out the specific details. This generally takes a week or two.

Assuming that signing the Purchase and Sales Agreement goes smoothly, your partners officially have the property under contract. Now it's time to put some skin in the game (earnest money) and pop the hood on the property (due diligence) to see what's lurking inside.

AT-RISK MONEY

Earnest money is a token amount of capital the sponsors deposit into escrow to signify the buyer's good faith intent to purchase the property. It's effectively putting a hold on the asset while the sponsors arrange for financing and execute due diligence. The amount of earnest money is usually between 0.5 and 1% of the purchase price (a significant amount of money when acquiring properties worth tens of millions of dollars).

Prospective buyers who want to make their deal particularly enticing might offer to put up more earnest money. This is one way of helping an offer stand out amongst the competition during the LOI phase. Usually the earnest money is refundable should the buyer back out of the deal during the due diligence period. If they back out after this contingency period expires, on the other hand, they'll forfeit the deposit.

Backing out even a single day after due diligence has expired means potentially losing hundreds of thousands of dollars. Ouch.

This is just one of the many risks the sponsors assume in the process of acquiring an asset.

DUE DILIGENCE

Every year I visit my doctor for one of the most awkward hours of my life: my annual physical.

During this hour, the doctor asks probing personal questions about how I'm feeling, how I've been sleeping or eating or exercising or... you name it, he asks it.

In a perfect world, the doctor could rely exclusively on my answers to these questions. This, however, is not a perfect world and the doctor knows that patients are 1) prone to lying and 2) not omniscient.

So this is where things get weird. The doctor asks me to strip down and put on a thin sheet that they give the elegant title of "gown." Then the doctor feels me up in all sorts of uncomfortable ways. Poking this and then prodding that.

Despite the awkward discomfort of it all, I return each and every year. Why? Because I can't know all the things potentially going wrong in my body.

An apartment building is a lot like a human. The roof, siding, and foundation are a type of skin, while the boiler, HVAC, and water heater are awfully similar to organs. Electrical wiring functions like a nervous system, and plumbing is pretty much no different from a digestive system.

When we buy a building, it's not enough to simply ask the owner for everything that's going wrong. Remember, humans lie. Sometimes unintentionally, sometimes not. Also, just as you can't look at a person and know if their arteries are a ticking time bomb, a quick glance at a building isn't enough to know if it's on the fast-track to cardiac arrest.

This is where due diligence comes in, and it's a lot like a physical.

Once a property goes under contract, the deal sponsor has limited time to mobilize a fleet of specialists to crawl over every inch of the building. It's during this period that we're challenging the assumptions made during underwriting to either corroborate or invalidate our projections. The ultimate goal of due diligence is to ensure there are no unexpected surprises looming on the horizon.

There's a lot that goes into conducting thorough due diligence, and all of this work falls squarely on the sponsor's shoulders. Still, passive investors should understand enough of what's expected during this process that they can ask the right questions of the deal sponsor.

The length of due diligence is negotiable, but it's usually between ten and sixty days. This is the time to decide whether to take a deal to closing. Generally, there's no consequence (besides potential reputational damage) to backing out of a deal during due diligence. Earnest money will be returned and everybody goes their merry way.

Exiting *after* the due diligence period has ended, on the other hand, carries some potentially significant penalties, including forfeiture of the earnest money. This is a tough pill to swallow, but sometimes it can't be avoided.

It's imperative that the sponsors move quickly and efficiently during this period to answer any lingering questions about a deal's potential viability.

To gauge whether to pull the plug and run, the deal sponsor will conduct two forms of due diligence: **physical** and **financial**.

PHYSICAL DUE DILIGENCE

This is what most people think of when it comes to due diligence. During physical due diligence, we walk every square inch of a property with our team of experts (engineers, plumbers, architects, electricians, property managers, etc.) to discover any potential surprises and ensure that the building's physical state is in alignment with our underwritten expectations.

The sponsors also use this time to sharpen their underwriting and dial in their business plan. Often operators only have sixty days (at maximum) to close a deal, and a lot of things have to happen concurrently. Raising capital takes time, so the sponsors will usually start conversations with investors before due diligence is completed and the final numbers are solidified. The sponsor should inform you of that fact and update projections as new information becomes available.

It's also during this period that the bank will have the building appraised by a third party. The appraisal attempts to peg a property's fair-market value. This can prove critical if the valuation comes back lower than expected. You might think twice before purchasing a building for more than what the bank thinks it's worth (the bank sure will).

Obviously physical due diligence is a critical step toward making sure we aren't walking into a complete money pit, but there's another part of due diligence that's equally important: financial due diligence.

FINANCIAL DUE DILIGENCE

Here's a critical reminder: *numbers can be made to lie.*

That probably just got a bunch of match nerds lathered up into a red-hot rage, but it's true. Numbers are only as good as the humans wielding them, and humans are fallible. Even well-intentioned humans can accidentally manipulate inputs in ways that lead to desired outputs.

This is obviously problematic. The solution?

First, educate yourself on the underwriting process. Second, only invest with trustworthy operators.

You don't need to know everything about underwriting, just enough to know when something doesn't look quite right. The best safeguard against questionable underwriting practices is to avoid doing business with unscrupulous and inexperienced operators.

Speaking of unscrupulous individuals, I'm not suggesting all sellers can't be trusted, but... Okay, fine, that's exactly what I'm saying. Sellers can't be trusted. Neither can brokers.

The operator's responsibility is to vet every assumption and piece of information provided by the seller. This is called financial due diligence and it occurs when the operators get their hands on these key documents:

- Rent roll

- T-12s

- Profit and Loss (P&L) statements

- Certificate of occupancy

- Environmental reports

- Current service contracts

- Outstanding bills

- Active and pending litigations

- Insurance loss run

- Maintenance records

- Notices of violations

- Title report

- Utility bills

During financial due diligence, we're verifying the accuracy of the numbers we've based our projections upon. Depending on the types of deals your operator is targeting, it's not uncommon for mom-and-pop sellers to have kept pretty abysmal records over the years.

This doesn't signal anything sinister, just incompetence—which is often one of the reasons these properties are attractive in the first place. A mismanaged property is typically full of unrealized value. But it also means being extra diligent during this process.

CAPITAL RAISING

The moment the ink dries on the Purchase and Sales Agreement, the sponsors should be going into capital-raising mode. Most projects will close within sixty days (or less) of signing the PSA.

That's not a ton of time to raise a couple million dollars in capital.

If you're a prospective passive investor who's established a substantive preexisting relationship with an operator, then expect to be informed of the deal within a week of the property going under contract. You'll receive a marketing package via email, plus information about an upcoming investor webinar.

No matter how much reading or preparing you've done, you'll be surprised by how quickly things move once that first deal comes across your desk. Deals often close in less than sixty days, while the funding window is generally much shorter.

If you've only ever invested in the stock market, you might be shocked by how quickly these offerings fill up. Apartment syndications are popular investment opportunities. Unfortunately, great deals aren't growing on trees, and there's often more capital sitting on the sidelines looking for a home than there are great deals.

It's simple supply and demand.

When a deal *does* arrive, savvy investors don't waste time taking action. This is problematic for new investors who might be hesitant to pull the trigger on their first deal. This is understandable. It's also why we encourage investors to spend so much time educating themselves before a deal becomes available.

Knowledge breeds confidence. That you're reading this book now suggests you're ahead of that curve. By the time you encounter your first marketing package, you're unlikely to feel hopelessly overwhelmed, but still… it's daunting. Anxiety is born from not knowing what's going to happen next. So let's alleviate some of that anxiety by breaking down the funding timeline.

ATTRACTIVE DEAL ARRIVES: START THE CLOCK

Day 0–7

Finally, an awesome-looking deal arrives on your desk, usually in the form of a digital marketing package. From here, most sponsors host an investment presentation, webinar, or one-on-one phone call. We're a fan of the webinar format because it gives you the opportunity to benefit from other investors' questions.

If you're interested in the deal, next is to place a *soft commitment*. This doesn't guarantee your placement in the offering, nor does it commit you to funding the deal. The soft commitment simply conveys your interest to the operator so they can gauge the progress of the raise.

Next, you'll receive the private placement memorandum (PPM) once it's been assembled by the lawyers (which is usually within a few days of the webinar).

Days 7–28

With the PPM in hand, the ball is now in your court to make a decision and deliver funds.

Syndications fill up quickly on a first-come-first-serve basis. Signing the paperwork isn't enough. Making a pinky promise isn't enough either. Your place in an offering is not secured until your money has been received, and even then there's the possibility that the offering becomes oversubscribed and somebody gets kicked out.

Expect to sign the PPM and transfer funds within two to three weeks of first receiving news of the deal.

Days 28–42

Closing takes place within one to two weeks of the funding deadline. Experienced operators might schedule the funding deadline even further out from closing, as they know that nothing should be left to chance during this high-stress time. No deal sponsor wants to show up to the closing table without funds firmly in hand.

If your operator doesn't require funds in place at least a week before closing, then they've yet to experience all the ways the universe will conspire against them in the final moments of a deal. Pray they don't find out the hard way.

Once you've transferred your funds, the active portion of your role in the investment is officially complete. From this point on, the operator takes care of everything else and you're officially a passive investor. Congratulations!

Closing

Whether it's wired funds not arriving when expected or paperwork not landing where it should, every operator seems to have a closing table horror story.

This isn't terribly surprising, considering how many moving parts, ranging from the title company to the lawyers to the bank, are involved. None of this should hit the passive investor's radar, but be aware that the deal sponsors are juggling many balls during this period to ensure everything crosses the finish line smoothly.

Your role in the closing procedures is to simply sit back and wait patiently for the call or email from your operator notifying you that everything has closed according to plan.

Once you receive word that the deal has closed, go ahead and celebrate. It's been a long road getting to this point! Your sponsors are due a small celebration as well, but for them the real work has only just begun.

So now you know understand the deal acquisition timeline. Funding your first syndication can be stressful and scary. Hopefully by understanding the exact timeline and step-by-step process, you can go into that first deal with eyes wide open and reduce the amount of overall stress and headache.

All told, it's a pretty simple process. Once you experience it for the first time, we think you'll agree. In fact, once you get a taste for how simple it is (and receive that first cash flow distribution), you'll be hooked.

And then it's time to start over and find another deal!

CHAPTER 19

INVESTMENT OFFERING SUMMARY

"Million-dollar ideas are worthless
without million-dollar execution."

- Anthony Vicino

My significant other once called me "pathologically frugal."

Sparks of anxiety fire in my gut whenever I contemplate a potential purchase, no matter how small. It often takes me months of working up the chutzpah to pull the trigger on an item that I *really* want. Unfortunately, once it arrives, I usually experience such debilitating buyer's remorse that I'll return the item after only having had it for a week.

It's rarely the product's fault.

It's a "me" thing.

Again, I'm pathologically frugal.

Sometimes, however, it's *not* my fault. Sometimes the product is absolutely nothing like what was advertised.

I recently made the mistake of trying to buy a suit online at one of those made-to-order websites, the type of place where you send in your own slapdash measurements and awkward photos taken in the living room with poor lighting, and somehow the tailor on the other end is expected to craft you a bespoke garment worthy of the red carpet.

Here's the problem: When buying an article of clothing on the internet, you don't have much to go off of except for the pictures and videos on the company's website. The sculpted models parading around in these outfits would look great in a burlap bag.

So you're left with a certain impression of how an outfit will look on *you* that's not necessarily tied to reality.

I kept this in mind while unboxing the suit I was hoping would move me three notches deeper into the James Bond–lookalike category. Instead, I came out looking like Mr. Bean. The sleeves were too long, the shoulders too boxy, the pants too wide. I felt like a little boy wearing his dad's suit.

While comparing the suit I'd received to the one advertised on the website, it became clear that these two things were about as different in reality as Vincent Van Gogh's *A Starry Night* is from a second grader's finger paintings on the refrigerator.

I felt lied to, deceived by the same sort of marketing magic that somehow makes a McDonald's burger look fresh and delicious when seen on a billboard.

Keep this in mind as you embark on the next phase of your passive investing journey and receive the investment offering summary. Make no mistake, this is a marketing package. It's designed to present the investment opportunity in the best light possible.

Now, every investment summary is a bit different. Some might be professionally arranged thirty-page documents with beautiful pictures, charts, and graphs. Others might be nothing more than a single page summary outlining a few basic highlights.

Neither approach is right or wrong. Don't be drawn in by the glitz and glamour of a shiny offering overcompensating for any lack of substance. Then again, a lazily assembled offering summary might be a sign of how that operator handles all aspects of their business.

This calls to mind a quote we use frequently around the office: **"She who is diligent with the small things can be entrusted with the big things."** We find this to be true in nearly all walks of life.

We believe professionalism and attention to detail matter, but you can't judge a book by its cover. You must dig deeper into the offering and challenge its assumptions to uncover whether it's a worthy deal or not.

The first step in doing so is to establish your investment criteria. By this point, you should have already established a set of guidelines and non-negotiable screening items you'll use to review an investment opportunity.

So with your investment parameters clearly in mind, let's review the sections you'll most commonly find in an investment offering to determine whether this is 1) a good deal and 2) a good deal for *you*.

Don't be afraid to ask hard questions while you probe this document. The last thing you want is to jump into a nightmare deal that only looks great on paper.

Quick note: This is an example of how *we* lay out information at Invictus Capital and is for educational purposes only. Presentation and information vary by operator. In general, these are the sections you can expect to find.

EXECUTIVE SUMMARY

The first section you'll encounter is a high-level deal overview that sets the table so anybody can understand the opportunity at a glance. Here you'll find condensed information on the team, the asset, and broad neighborhood or market highlights, plus a summary of what makes the deal attractive. You'll often find the piece of information most investors are eager to see: return projections.

This page, funneled through the filter of your personal investment parameters, should give you enough information to make a snap decision as to whether the opportunity is worth learning more about. Here are some questions to consider:

- *Are the projected returns in alignment with your expectations?*

- *Is the business plan consistent with your goals?*

- *Is the property consistent with your desired asset class, vintage, or quality?*

- *Geographically, is this in an area you've done due diligence on?*

Even if *that* deal doesn't make sense for your particular goals, it can still prove useful to dive in to the rest of the package, if for no other reason than to glean deeper insight into the mind and underwriting practices of the deal sponsor. More data points on an operator are never a bad thing.

INVESTMENT HIGHLIGHTS

The Investment Highlights delivers a more detailed glimpse into what makes this deal so uniquely attractive.

Perhaps you'll discover information about a particularly juicy return structure favoring the limited partners, or some insider information about the underlying market conditions. This section offers a broad-strokes explanation of the business plan and strategy to be employed. If this is a value-add opportunity, for example, how exactly does the operator intend to force appreciation? Is there room to increase rents, or are there any glaring operational inefficiencies?

The IRR, cash-on-cash, annualized return, and target hold period are also usually represented here. And finally, you'll often find an example return structure outlining projected investor earnings based on an investment amount of around $100,000. Most investors simply want to know how much they stand to make without having to do complicated math. This section should provide that.

THE BUSINESS PLAN

You probably know somebody with a killer business idea that they've been talking about for years. Despite all the talk, they don't have much to show for their efforts. In fact, it doesn't even seem like they have much of a plan.

Then again, how many businesses *with a plan* fail in their first couple years? In our experience, it's less about the quality of the plan and more to do with the quality of the execution. This section of the marketing package details how *exactly* the operator plans to deliver all those stunning projected returns outlined on the previous pages.

Is this a value-add or development deal? Will it require heavy improvements to mechanicals or simply a cosmetic face-lift coupled with tenant turnover?

You must understand the *story* behind the deal. It's easy to get lost in the cold, unfeeling numbers. If you want to confuse somebody, throw a ton of numbers and data at them. In most instances, the other person won't bother interjecting (even if they're confused) for fear of looking stupid.

Numbers and data are helpful, but our squishy human brains aren't evolved to process numbers. We process stories.

When we hear the *story* behind the deal, we're much better able to pinpoint the sections that don't make sense. Our subconscious and intuition kick in to find the plot holes. And trust me, you're an expert at finding the plot holes. You've been consuming stories since you were a baby.

For instance, let's present a piece of information and see which is easier to understand on a hundred-unit apartment building with some heavy value-add potential: numbers or stories.

1. We project 20% year one rent growth after completing upgrades on half the units. We will maintain 95% occupancy and deliver a 10% cash-on-cash return, which will be paid out starting the first full quarter after close.
2. Currently half of the units are renting 20% below market due to outdated units. Our plan is to renovate all fifty outdated units in the first quarter after closing. Because of the strong rental demand in this area and the newly renovated units, we'll achieve 95% occupancy by the beginning of the second quarter and will begin distributing quarterly returns of 10% cash-on-cash.

Despite both narratives presenting the exact same information, the first version requires more heavy mental lifting. That first version gives numbers and data that we must then process contextually before we can judge whether the plan is sound. The story version gives us not only the data, but also fills in the context so we don't have to do that ourselves.

As a result, we have more mental bandwidth free to ask some important questions, such as:

- When do the leases for these fifty tenants expire? Does that conveniently (and somewhat magically) occur in the first quarter after close? If not, how are you intending to get all those tenants out?

- Even if all fifty units were vacant from day one, do you have the construction team capable of turning fifty units that quickly?

- Supposing you had fifty vacant units and flipped them within ninety days, is it realistic to expect you could instantaneously lease them out to achieve the projected 10% CoC return?

I don't know about you, but even just asking those questions makes me suspicious of this deal being unrealistic.

> *"You must not fool yourself—and you are the easiest person to fool."*
>
> — Richard Feynman

In an attempt not to fool myself, here's the question I ask whenever I evaluate a deal: **How realistic is this really?**

Always consider how many assumptions must be wrong (and wrong by how much) before the deal gets into trouble.

Again, it's relatively easy to make the numbers show whatever you want them to. It's in finding the story and applying common sense that we can determine if this million-dollar idea is actually executable.

If you're still not able to answer these questions after reading this section of the marketing package, it might be time to get the operator on the phone to explain. Sometimes just hearing the story come out of somebody else's mouth can tell you everything you need to know.

THE TEAM

If you've been paying attention throughout this book, you know how we feel about vetting operators. If you blacked out for a bit, no worries, let me reiterate. *Vetting operators is a passive investor's most important job.*

By the time you receive the marketing package, you've already thoroughly vetted the operator, so it's unlikely this section will reveal anything you don't already know.

MARKET OVERVIEW

Just as you have already vetted the operator before getting to this point, you should have also done research on this prospective market before now.

This section should only reinforce what you already know about the macro-market, but as the cliche goes, **"Real estate is all about location, location, location."** That applies at the macro-metropolitan level all the way down to the specific neighborhood level.

It's that latter bit of information you're keying in on in this section.

How's the neighborhood's crime, median income, vacancy, and median rent? Also, what sorts of new development trends is this area forecasting?

Unless you're investing in a city you're already familiar with (and possibly living in), it's unlikely you have all the neighborhoods in a non-local city memorized. That's all right. By the end of this section in the marketing package, you should have a sufficient understanding of the neighborhood in question.

PROPERTY OVERVIEW

Now it's time for the down and dirty details of the property itself.

- How many buildings?

- What's the vintage or age of the buildings?

- How many units?

- What's the unit mix? (i.e. How many one-, two-, or three-bed-room units?)

- What's the average square footage per unit?

Also, expect to find pictures of both the exterior and interior in this section. Look for photos of bathrooms and kitchens in particular. These are two of the easiest places an operator can add value by improving appliances, floors, and fixtures.

INVESTMENT SUMMARY

For the numbers nerds out there, a lot can be gleaned from the investment summary. In fact, Dan flips straight to this section when evaluating a new opportunity. It's here that he finds the underwriting assumptions coupled with details of the debt structure that he can pass through his experience filter to determine whether a deal warrants more consideration.

We don't recommend this technique for newer investors. It's too easy to sell yourself on a deal based on juicy projected returns without first knowing the story.

Some important areas of the investment summary to pay attention to are:

Purchase Price

We've talked a lot about how the value of a commercial property is deter-mined by the formula NOI / Cap Rate = Building Value. With that said, buildings of a certain size, vintage, and location, will trade roughly in the same range.

In our market, the Twin Cities, Class B properties trade at around $120–180k/unit. To arrive at this number, simply divide the total purchase price by the number of units. This is a handy at-a-glance metric that can give you an idea of where this property is trading relative to other properties in the area.

Occupancy

There isn't a good or bad number to see here. A high occupancy could be a great thing if the business plan indicates you are acquiring a stabilized asset with a good tenant base. A high vacancy rate, by comparison, could also be desirable, assuming the business plan calls for the operator to vacate the building for large-scale redevelopment. This occupancy number is only good or bad relative to the presented business plan.

Cap Rate and Projected Exit Cap Rate

This singular assumption might be the most important in the entire document when it comes to assessing the conservative or aggressive nature of an operator's underwriting.

The cap rate can skew a building's valuation more than any other number. A skewed valuation leads to skewed return projections. It's critical to apply conservative assumptions when forecasting future cap rates at time of disposition.

Everybody's crystal ball is equally murky. Predicting macro-market states at any point in the future is dubious at best. The operators who survive the longest are the ones who expect the future to be at least slightly worse than the present.

A good rule of thumb is to expect the projected exit cap rate to be higher at the time of disposition than at the time of purchase. Of course, this suppresses the projected returns, but under-promising and over-delivering is better than the alternative.

Debt Terms

The most important partner is the one bringing the majority of the capital.

That's the bank in most real estate deals. At minimum, you should understand the broad strokes of the debt being used to purchase a property.

Equity Available

Here you'll learn how much total capital is required to close the deal, along with the minimum and maximum investment amounts.

Why would there be a maximum investment amount? Because the bank will underwrite any single investor contributing over a certain threshold (say 20%). That could also mean the individual or entity will be required to guarantee the loan alongside the deal sponsors.

If you're all right taking on the additional risk, then you can probably work out a deal with the sponsors to contribute over the maximum.

INVESTMENT FORECAST AND RETURN PROJECTIONS

If you're all about the numbers, you'll enjoy this section. If (like most sane people) you don't wake up every morning thinking about numbers and spreadsheets, well, then this section can still be pretty enjoyable.

Okay, "enjoyable" is overselling things. Regardless, this section is important, so you'll have to endure.

These sections break down the proforma profit and loss statement, often in great detail.

There are many golden nuggets to be plucked from this section. The most valuable of all is deeper insight into the mind of your operator and how they underwrite. You'll see firsthand, in the data, the sorts of assumptions they've made to arrive at their projected returns.

While combing through this section, keep Mark Twain's words at the front of your mind: **"There are three types of lies: lies, damned lies, and statistics."**

Don't take the numbers on this page for granted. Challenge them for yourself to find the truth.

In this section, you'll see certain numbers that, when passed through the correct filters, will reveal the truth of the investment. As a quick reminder, the filters and assumptions to pay particular attention to are rent growth, expense growth, exit cap rate, vacancy, and the operational expense ratio.

BENEFITS OF INVESTING

This is usually a sales pitch of some sort rehashing the many benefits of real estate investing. This could include more information on the equity splits, preferred returns, advanced tax strategies, distribution schedules, and so on.

TIMELINE

By the time investors receive a polished marketing package, the clock has started ticking and the operators have officially boarded a crazy-train that's fast approaching the closing date.

If you're interested in funding the deal, pay close attention to when the funds must be received. If the operator has requested a soft commitment, quickly notify them of your interest. This does not reserve or guarantee your place in the deal, nor does it commit you to funding the deal.

Because private placements are such highly sought-after investment opportunities, you must move quickly to deliver your funds. It's not uncommon for capital raises to close within forty-eight hours of the investor presentation. Drag your feet and you'll miss out on the opportunity altogether.

If this is your first deal, the pace at which things suddenly move can feel overwhelming. That's understandable. This is why it's important to put in the time now to educate yourself on the process, vet your operator, and prepare funds for transfer. That way, when that unicorn deal finally crosses your desk, you'll be able to move forward quickly and confidently.

RENTAL AND SALES COMPARABLES

You can't reasonably project how much value can be added to a property until you understand the current market conditions. It's important to have a baseline against which to compare the underwriting assumptions. If the sponsor says in-place rents are 20% below market, they must substantiate the claim. To validate market claims, we'll need two reports showing rental and sales comparables.

Rental comps show how much similar units within a particular area are currently renting for, whereas the sales comp tells what similar buildings have sold for in the recent past. These reports can be derived from CoStar, current Craigslist ads, or the tried-and-true method of secret-shopping the competition.

Both bits of information are helpful in determining how conservative or liberal the sponsors have been in constructing their business plan.

Are they targeting rent premiums that would land them in the top 10% of units renting in a particular neighborhood?

When they say they're purchasing the building for less than market value, are they using the mean, median, or mode to make that declaration?

These things matter and can easily skew assumptions, so don't gloss over this section. Even if you end up passing on this deal, understanding the comps in an MSA is helpful for analyzing future opportunities.

WEBINAR OR PHONE CALL

After receiving the marketing package, the deal sponsor will typically host some sort of investor webinar, phone call, or dinner to present the deal in more detail and to answer any questions you might have. I've yet to find a marketing package so fantastic that it left me without any follow-up questions.

Even if I were presented with the unicorn deal package and had zero questions, I would still hop on a call or attend the webinar so I could hear the story of the deal from the operators themselves.

You might look through quite a few marketing packages and attend an equal number of investor webinars before finally pulling the trigger on that first deal. There's nothing wrong with that.

Investing is a long-term game. Move at whatever pace feels right to you and ignore that most pernicious of feelings: *the fear of missing out.* There's always another deal around the corner. Never feel the pressure to jump into a once-in-a-lifetime opportunity.

If, however, you've found a rock-star operator, they've presented you with a killer opportunity, and you're ready to take the plunge... Well, then it's time to bring in the legal beagles, 'cause next up, we're diving into the private placement memorandum (PPM).

CHAPTER 20

THE PRIVATE PLACEMENT MEMORANDUM

"To me, a lawyer is basically the person that knows the rules of the country. We're all throwing the dice, playing the game, moving our pieces around the board, but if there is a problem the lawyer is the only person who has read the inside of the top of the box."

— Jerry Seinfeld

The private placement memorandum (PPM) is a highly technical and hefty document filled with legal jargon and disclaimers designed to scare pretty much anyone out of investing. In anything. Ever.

Distilled to its essence, the PPM's goal is to inform you of all the inherent risks associated with a particular investment.

It's a riveting read if you love legalese. If not, then it's quite the chore. Because it's so dense with legalese, it's highly advisable you have your own lawyer take a look.

With that said, the PPM is critically important and you should also read it yourself. This document is there to protect you (the investor) and to enable you to make a well-informed decision about the investment opportunity by equipping you with all the necessary information. Don't pass responsibility for reading this document entirely to your lawyer.

To make your task easier, let's demystify this document and make it simpler to navigate.

PPMs vary by the type of issuer, the size of the offering, the number and type of investors being solicited, and the individual lawyer assembling the document. At their core, each private placement memorandum contains these six sections: Executive Summary, Summary of Terms, Risk Factors, Operating Agreement, Asset Management Agreement, Subscription Agreement, Investor Qualification Form, and Signatures Page.

1) Executive Summary

This section is usually a copy-pasted version of the marketing package. If the deal doesn't have a marketing package, then expect a condensed description of the investment here, including pricing information, minimum subscription amount, investor qualifications, and management fees.

2) Summary of Terms

The Summary of Terms (a.k.a. the *Confidential Term Sheet*) is a cornucopia of useful definitions. Let's focus on a few of the more useful sections.

First, a breakdown of the actual share classes. Most commonly, these are Series A Units (investor shares) and Series B Units (managing member shares). Ownership of these shares will break down along the lines of the equity split (70/30, for example). Here you'll also find a reminder of the minimum and maximum investment size for limited partners, plus insight into how much the managing members (GP) intend to co-invest in the deal.

Next, Distribution Rights outlines the return structure for each of the groups (limited partners and general partners). Any preferred return or complicated waterfall structure will be detailed here. It's helpful to spend a little extra time on this section to understand how returns are calculated.

Now we come to an important section for understanding the deal sponsor's compensation: Management Fees and Expenses.

What fees will the general partners collect in conjunction with their efforts? The most common fees you'll find are acquisition, asset management, loan guarantor, refinance, and disposition fees.

There is no shortage of ways to structure fees in a syndication. With that said, look for fee structures tied to the overall performance of an asset. We have a problem with sponsors earning fees regardless of how poorly the project performs.

Nip this potential issue in the bud by giving the fees and equity structure some deep consideration before jumping into a deal destined only to deliver great returns to the general partners.

3) Risk Factors

If this were the only section you bothered reading, you probably wouldn't invest in anything ever again. This section outlines all the worst-case doom-and-gloom scenarios.

The purpose of the Risk Factors section isn't to scare you out of investing, though. It's merely making certain you're fully aware of the many ways a deal could fail to perform.

You'll find all of the risk factors that you'd encounter in pretty much any investment opportunity, plus all of the risk factors associated with *that* deal specifically.

Investing is inherently risky. There's no such thing as a guaranteed return. If you don't realize that after reading this section, then you weren't paying close enough attention.

4) Operating Agreement

Now we arrive at the real meat and potatoes of the private placement memorandum. The Operating Agreement is a densely packed smorgasbord of legalese. If you don't have a legal background, it might prove difficult to get through.

But persist you must, for in these hallowed pages you will discover priceless information about the *rules of the game*. Or, put another way, about how the underlying business will actually operate.

I get it, you're busy and not keen on reading dry legal contracts. This is where a lawyer comes in handy (and yes, if you remember from the earlier chapter on how to build a rock-star team, you absolutely should have a lawyer reviewing the PPM before you sign).

Still, even if you pass the proverbial football over to your lawyer, you should still take a crack at perusing this section, as it answers many of the most commonly asked questions. This is a tedious process at first, but after a couple of deals, you'll gain familiarity with the document and know precisely what to look for on future opportunities.

5) Asset Management Agreement

The Asset Management Agreement designates who exactly the asset manager is, all the responsibilities of that role, and the compensation structure for that person or group. Most deal sponsors hold their ownership interest in a syndication through a separate *managing LLC*. This intermediary company is often assigned the role of asset manager.

The asset manager works directly with the property management team to ensure key performance indicators are achieved and the business plan is executed successfully. Also, they handle all tax and legal issues, including annual distribution of investor K-1s. This person is your point of contact handling investor communications and quarterly or annual updates about the status of the asset.

6) Subscription Agreement, Investor Qualifications Form, and Signatures Page

It's time to make some actual commitments.

Up to this point, everything in the PPM has been informational, with nothing for *you* to sign. That changes with the Subscription Agreement, Investor Qualification Form, and Signatures Page.

First, the Subscription Agreement is where you'll signal how many shares of the company you intend to purchase. Usually this is just a blank line for you to fill in.

Second, through the Investor Qualification Form you'll designate your investor status.

Third, on the Signatures Page you'll provide your personal information in the form of name and address. Also, you'll detail how exactly you plan to hold ownership in the company. This could be individually or through some sort of tenants in common, partnership, LLC, corporation, trust or estate, or IRA.

Unsure which box to tick? Talk to your lawyer or CPA.

Let's circle back to that Investor Qualification Form real quick. This part can be a tad confusing depending on the type of offering.

In the case of a 506(b) offering, you'll self-select your status. Tick the box of the description corresponding most closely with your financial situation and sophistication, then tick that box.

It's not quite as simple in a 506(c) offering, which only allows accredited investors to participate. In this structure, a higher level of verification is required. This is handled either by a third-party service or through your broker, attorney, or certified accountant. Because there are more hoops to jump through in the verification process, most operators opt for the 506(b) structure, which creates less headache for the passive investors.

If at any point you're confused or have questions, do yourself a favor and speak to your lawyer. We've pounded the talk-to-your-lawyer drum a whole lot in this chapter, but this is where rubber meets road. Real estate syndications are illiquid assets. Once you're in a deal, you're locked in with these operators for at least a couple years. Don't cut corners at the finish line hoping it'll all work out.

Hope is not a viable investment strategy.

If you think you'll save a couple bucks by cutting out a lawyer at this point in the journey, think again, penny pincher. There's a good chance you're going to lose even more in the long run.

The two things you don't skimp on when it comes to investing are legal and tax advice. A good lawyer (and CPA) will save you more money than they cost. Get them involved in the process. It'll be the best investment you ever make

Yes, even better than an investment in multifamily.

CHAPTER 21

WHAT TO EXPECT AFTER YOU INVEST

*"The single biggest problem in communication
is the illusion that it has taken place."*

— George Bernard Shaw

Congratulations, you've invested in an apartment syndication!

Now what?

Depending on the business plan, you're often looking at a hold period of somewhere between five and seven years. So what should you do during this time?

Well, honestly... not much. You're a passive investor, after all. You did your part. You funded the deal. Now it's time to sit back and collect mailbox money, right?

Wrong.

You've got to keep a finger on the pulse of the project to ensure the sponsors are doing their job. That pulse should come through regular communications with the operators.

If you don't stay up to date and mentally checked-in during a project, you can find yourself in the position of one of our investors (to protect the innocent, we'll call him Gary), whose first passive investment with an operator ended catastrophically.

That might seem an extreme word choice, but what else do you call it when the deal sponsor loses all of your money?

So what did Gary's first deal sponsor do so wrong?

Well, for starters, the operator never did any of the renovations as projected. Second, he fled the country.

How on Earth could such a thing happen, and what could Gary have done differently?

From what I understand, this operator was actually fairly communicative in the beginning. Although they were often vague on details, the sponsor did issue quarterly updates and often answered the phone when called. At some point, however, the renovations started falling behind.

Anybody who's ever worked a construction project knows these things often run over budget and over time. If not properly managed, this creates a snowball effect of horribleness.

Gary's operator didn't stop the snowball while it was still small. In the end, it ran him over. Overwhelmed and panicked, this deal sponsor decided the most prudent course of action was to simply run away. It took nearly nine months for anybody to notice.

Incompetence is often worse than malice.

To protect your interests in the project, stay involved and mentally engaged. Carefully review the communications provided, question the assumptions made, and challenge anything that doesn't feel right.

With that in mind, here are the most common communications you can expect to receive throughout the life of a project.

AFTER THE CLOSE

Regular Communications

Expect regular updates (often monthly) at the start of a project, when the property is undergoing the heaviest renovations and repositioning.

You'll want to see signs that the operator is executing the business plan as anticipated. These communications typically focus on general status updates on vacancy metrics, unit turns in progress/completed, and projected versus actual collections.

Frequent monthly communications become less necessary once the asset is stabilized. At this point, you might only receive quarterly and annual updates.

Apartment syndications aren't like buying stocks through an app on your phone, where you can check their performance with the push of a button. The amount of information the limited partners receive is entirely dependent on what the sponsors make available.

Ask for examples of previous investor communications before deciding to work with a sponsor. This'll help ensure everybody is on the same page about what will be communicated and when, well before the deal begins.

The most valuable information you're looking for in these communications has nothing to do with how many air conditioners were replaced last month or how many vacancies the property currently has. What you should care most about is how the property is performing relative to the business plan.

Don't be bamboozled by operators who create new annual budgets and business plans against which to judge the year's performance. Don't let operators move the goalpost each year. What you want to see are performance numbers measured against the projections that were presented to you at the start of the deal.

Operators don't always draw these conclusions so clearly and cleanly for you, especially if the deal isn't performing well. You might have to do some comparative analysis yourself.

Annual Communications

Every year you'll receive a K-1 tax form detailing how much you made or lost in the previous calendar year. You'll need this for tax purposes. You should see depreciation reducing your taxable income on the investment.

Now, there are a few moving parts involved in preparing taxes. If you're working with an operator who doesn't have their act together at the beginning of the year, you might find yourself without a K-1 as the tax deadline fast approaches. If this happens, you'll have to file for an extension.

If you've never done a private placement before, don't be surprised if the K-1 is the last piece of the tax puzzle you're waiting on each year. Preparing these documents takes longer than most people anticipate. Generally you should expect to have your K-1 within ninety days of closing the year (around the end of March).

Cash Flow Distributions

Most projects issue cash flow distributions either monthly or quarterly via ACH or check. Some investors prefer the regularity and consistency of monthly distributions. Often these investors are relying on this income for living expenses. Other investors without an immediate need for the capital are usually fine with quarterly distributions.

Which camp you fall into depends upon your particular circumstances.

If this is something that matters to you, it's definitely worth asking the operator how frequently they make distributions *before* funding a deal.

Capital Event/Disposition Communications

Most value-add multifamily deals last three to seven years. During that time, there may arise the opportunity for a cash-out refinance.

If this occurs, you'll receive back a significant portion of your initial invested capital. The deal sponsor should notify you before executing a refinance or sale.

Capital Call

In life, and investing, there are countless ways things can go wrong.

A project may underperform due to poor management, inaccurate projections, massive market disruption, or from simply being under-capitalized from the beginning. There may come a time when the project is poised on the brink of disaster and, without a fresh infusion of capital, everybody stands to lose.

What comes next is a capital call, and it's every operator's worst nightmare. To save the deal, the sponsor must somehow bring more capital to the table. There are a couple ways this can be done.

First, if the operator is in a position to, they may put more of their own money into the deal. This might be considered a loan or purchase of equity. If it's a purchase of equity, then the question limited partners need answered is whether this dilutes their ownership position in the company.

Second, the operator can raise capital from an outside source. If this happens, it almost certainly dilutes your ownership position. Still, if the capital is required for the project to survive, it's usually better in the long run to own less of a performing deal than it is to own more of a completely defunct deal.

Third, the operator can raise more capital from the pool of passive investors currently in the deal. Sometimes the capital call is presented in the operating agreement as a non-optional event for the limited partners. Be certain you understand the provisions surrounding a potential capital call before you fund a deal. You don't want to discover at some unfortunate point down the road that the operator has the ability to levy penalties against limited partners who fail to answer the capital call.

From our perspective, there is no good justification for punishing the limited partners in this instance. You should be cautious of working with any deal sponsor who penalize investors for their own faulty projections.

Now, if you stay in the game long enough, a project will eventually fail to perform as expected. Unforeseeable macro-economic events slam the industry on occasion. If you receive the dreaded call from your deal sponsor asking for more capital, it shouldn't come as a complete surprise, assuming they've been forthright in their monthly/quarterly communications.

The best advice we have for navigating any failing business venture is to ask the question: **Can this be salvaged?** If not, resist the urge to throw good money after bad.

PARTING WORDS

These are the regular communications to expect from your operator. Throughout the life of a project, your ongoing duty is to hold the sponsors accountable to the projections they set from the beginning.

Compare their monthly and quarterly reports against their initial underwriting assumptions. Most operators won't balk to present this information when the deal is performing well. When a deal is struggling, well, some operators suddenly take the stance "less is more."

If something doesn't add up, or it seems the project isn't on the intended course, ask questions.

Investing, like life, isn't always rainbows and sunshine. Sometimes it rains. And when it does, you want a proactive operator who grabs an umbrella and does what needs doing.

This means proactive, honest communication both when things are going well, and, more importantly, when things aren't. It's during these periods that you gain truly meaningful insight into the character and quality of your partners.

What happens if the sponsors are doing an abysmal job and driving the project into the ground? Fingers crossed you never experience this nightmare. If you do, it's time to turn to the operating agreement to brush up on the provisions overseeing replacing the managing partner. There's usually language in the operating agreement making this possible in theory, although quite difficult to execute in reality.

In the worst-case scenario, you won't have a way to remove the sponsors. This is why it's so important you do the extra work required on the front end of a project to vet the sponsor for competency and integrity.

PART SEVEN

THE END

CHAPTER 22

THE END IS ONLY THE BEGINNING

"A story has no beginning or end: arbitrarily one chooses that moment of experience from which to look back or from which to look ahead."

— Graham Greene

Take a moment and give yourself a pat on the back.

You've taken the first step toward making your financial goals a reality. It might not seem like much, but you've done something incredible, something the vast majority of people in this world will never do. You've applied yourself diligently toward learning a subject that, at first glance, can seem downright terrifying and overwhelming.

Do you remember the first lesson we shared at the start of this journey together? It was this: *real estate investing is not terribly complicated.*

Now, be honest, when you first read those words you probably thought we were blowing smoke. The truth is, passive investing in apartment syndications is pretty darn simple.

Just think about how much you've learned over the past couple hundred pages. We started by plotting a course toward financial freedom. Most people never even stop to consider where they're going or whether the path they're on will get them there. But not you.

If you've done the work, you now have clarity on your *why*, your goals, and the investment parameters that will help you achieve the vision you have for your life.

After laying the foundation, we explored why multifamily assets are such powerful investment vehicles, what the heck a syndication is, how the business models works, and what your role is as a passive investor in the process.

Think about how much further ahead you are than the average person walking down the street who has no clue what a syndication is or how it can help them toward achieving their financial goals. You now possess a piece of rarefied information.

Unfortunately, it's not enough to *know* about the thing. You have to know what to do and how to do it. To that end, you've learned exactly what to look for in a deal sponsor, and how to be certain they're an all-star before you hand over your hard-earned money. Also, you've learned the invaluable skills of selecting a market and underwriting potential deals.

The point of all this education is to breed competence, which in turn leads to confidence. Confidence that you can then deploy against your next investment opportunity.

Let's not get it twisted, dear reader. Knowledge alone is not power. It's potential power. Without action, knowledge sits dormant and wasted.

The path forward is simple, but don't mistake that for being easy. None of the things worth having in life come easily. Life's rewards are earned through diligent execution.

You have the plans, the tools, and the knowledge necessary to invest in multifamily apartment syndications, but your journey to financial freedom, to getting off the stock market roller-coaster, and to building generational wealth has only just begun.

Now it's time to do the actual work.

Are you ready?

FREQUENTLY ASKED QUESTIONS

Can I invest in a syndication with retirement funds?

Absolutely. In fact, investing retirement funds through a self-directed IRA is one of the most common ways to passively invest in a real estate syndication.

The process of rolling a preexisting retirement account (401(k), IRA, 403b, etc.) into a self-directed IRA (SDIRA) is relatively simple and the fees are generally quite low. If you're looking for a great custodian, reach out to us through invictusmultifamily.com and we'll connect you with some great intermediaries.

Setting up an account only requires a bit of paperwork, but it can take a couple of weeks. If there's a particular deal you're interested in contributing funds to, best start the process sooner rather than later.

The actual process of funding a deal through an SDIRA is straightforward. Simply provide the custodian with copies of the legal documents from the private placement (PPM, operating agreement, and subscription agreement), and they will direct the funds on your behalf.

A couple things worth noting.

1. You can't take personal possession of the money at any point without incurring fees. This is why the custodian is necessary.
2. Talk with your CPA about any tax implications before making any decisions that could impact your financial situation.
3. Typically, you'll only be able to roll old retirement accounts from past employers into a self-directed IRA.

4. Special tax liabilities (UBIT and UDFI) will be incurred when investing in an asset utilizing leverage.

5. Certain transactions are restricted when utilizing a self-directed IRA. In particular, you cannot fund your own deal or the deal of a family member to whom you are related on the familial vertical axis (that means, parents, grandparents, children).

Last note, all returns flow back into the retirement account, so don't expect to live off the cash flow of a project if investing in this way.

Where do I find apartment syndication opportunities?

Because many apartment syndications cannot be publicly advertised, finding great opportunities can be difficult. The offerings you'll find publicly advertised are typically for accredited investors only.

Regardless, searching for deals is the wrong approach. First, find operators.

The best way to find opportunities is to get out to networking events, speak to other investors, and get referrals. The community of apartment syndicators is rather small, so once you get over the initial introductions with a few investors, the world of possibilities opens up.

Want to invest with Invictus Capital? Connect with us at www.invictus-multifamily.com.

Even if we're not a great fit for your investment goals, we can connect you with some rock-star operators who are!

How do private real estate syndications compare to real estate crowdfunding sites?

Real estate crowdfunding sites have become a popular way to passively invest in apartments.

It's an exciting new area that still feels a bit like the wild, wild west. Many big players have come and gone in only the few years this avenue has been available to the general public, so tread carefully.

Offerings through these channels can be presented in a number of ways, which may or may not allow for non-accredited investors.

From a high level, these online portals operate in one of two ways.

In the first, the portal itself is the sponsor, raising funds to be deployed in another operator's deal. This is similar to the role of capital raisers we discussed in an earlier chapter. In this arrangement, you won't have any interaction with the operating partner actually managing the property. All your communications, tax reports, and distributions will be handled through the crowdfunding platform.

There are two things we dislike about this structure.

The first obvious downside is the fact that you don't know the people running the deal. This makes vetting them difficult. In this instance, the crowdfunding portal is no different than if you were to invest in a faceless corporation through the stock market.

The second downside is that the crowdfunding portal is skimming additional fees that wouldn't be present had you gone directly to the managing operator. Now, one could say you are paying for the crowdfunding portal's expertise (in vetting operators), ease of use (in distributions and filings), and accessibility (you wouldn't have seen many of these opportunities otherwise), but that doesn't change the fact that now there's another middleman's mouth to feed.

The other way these portals operate is by merely serving as the connection point between you and the operating partner. This solves the first issue of not knowing the operator, though it doesn't change the second problem of additional fees. You might never directly see these fees (they're generally passed onto the operating partner), but you can bet those expenses will land somewhere in the underwriting.

None of this should dissuade you from exploring this option. Through these platforms you'll have access to offerings you couldn't find elsewhere. Be aware that many of the largest crowdfunding sites have come and gone (seemingly overnight), and that you'll be paying a bit more than you otherwise would if you went direct to the operators.

Our personal recommendation is that you spend the time and energy to network and find the operating partners yourself.

How much do I need to have to invest?

Minimum investment amounts vary by operator and by deal. We've seen minimums range anywhere between $5,000 all the way up to $500,000. Industry standard is usually around $50,000–$100,000.

How long will my money be tied up?

This largely depends on the asset type and business model. Average project life on a value-add multifamily opportunity is between five and seven years. There's always the possibility of an earlier exit, but keep in mind that real estate is an illiquid asset and that you shouldn't commit any funds that you might *need* in the next couple years.

Usually there are ways for an investor to exit a deal prematurely. They aren't easy, though, and usually mean taking a haircut on the returns to make it happen.

When does my preferred return start accruing? Does it roll over?

By now you understand that there are countless different ways to structure a syndication. It's important you understand the nuances of the unique deal in front of you.

One aspect to pay particular attention to is the preferred return. It's increasingly rare, in recent years, to find a deal that *doesn't* offer a preferred return. But remember, not all preferred returns are created equal.

First, when does the preferred return begin accruing?

Often it's day one, but not always. If the deal requires a heavy reposition or has a development component, there might not be any cash flow for the first year or two. You know if you're entering into a deal like this and shouldn't be surprised to find the delayed distribution of a preferred return.

Occasionally, however, you'll find operators who, regardless of how aggressive the property reposition is, do not start paying out the preferred return immediately. Get clear on this before funding the deal.

The second question to ask is whether the preferred return rolls over. For example, if a deal projecting an annual 8% preferred return only delivers 6% in year one, what happens to the remaining 2%? Does it disappear or does it roll over, to be made up in the subsequent years?

Industry standard, at the time of this writing, is for the preferred return to roll over until it's completely caught up.

Surely there are great deals that do not offer this, but you'd be hard-pressed to convince me to give them any money.

When should I expect my first distribution?

Again, this depends on the type of deal and the business plan being utilized.

Some projects are basic yield plays that start churning out cash from day one. Other projects might require a renovation and reposition taking upwards of six months, so distributions might be light until the project hits its stride in years two or three. On the far other end of the spectrum you have ground-up development deals, which might not generate any sort of return for up to five years.

Even within this diverse spectrum of project types, there are countless ways operators could handle distributions. They might be monthly or quarterly or annually or... you get the idea.

The most common distribution schedule for value-add multifamily projects is monthly or quarterly, beginning sometime within the first year of acquisition.

Can I roll my 1031 exchange into this deal?

That's a tricky question depending on a lot of factors unique to your situation. 1031 exchanges are a fantastic way to defer tax liabilities, but it's a needle that must be threaded precisely.

Technically, yes, there are ways you *could* roll a 1031 exchange into a syndication or a joint venture. This is most frequently done through a tenant in common (TIC) arrangement. Practically speaking, there's a lot of work and cost associated with going this route, and most operators aren't interested in jumping through all those hoops or incurring those expenses.

An interesting option worth considering in this instance is the Delaware Statutory Trust. DSTs are beyond the scope of this book, though it's worth looking into if you have a 1031 exchange in the foreseeable future.

Can I sell my shares early?

In many of the deals we've seen, there are ways for an investor to sell their shares prematurely (although this is by no means a given). Usually this takes form in one of three ways:

1. Sell your shares to the GP
2. Sell your shares to other LPs in the deal
3. Bring in a new investor into the deal to buy out your shares (with GP approval)

You should find the specific rules for early liquidation outlined in the Operating Agreement.

My recommendation to every investor posing this question is to come to terms with the fact that you're investing in an illiquid asset and that your money will be inaccessible for the duration of the hold. Go into the deal having mentally written off *needing* the money in any sort of shorter time span, and I promise you'll have a better investing experience overall.

What's the difference between a syndication and a REIT?

The Four Differences between a REIT and an Apartment Syndication

A while back, we sat down with a prospective passive investor to discuss a deal we were working on. He was excited about all the same things we get excited about when it comes to buying multifamily real estate.

The cash flow, the appreciation, the tax benefits, the control, the stability... he was psyched on all of it.

He went on to tell us that he loved investing in real estate so much that his portfolio was actually too heavily weighted in that sector and he was afraid of putting more money to work in that area. We were surprised to hear this because earlier in our conversation he'd made it clear he didn't own any real estate and that he'd never passively invested in a syndication.

We probed a bit deeper and discovered that he actually had nothing invested in real estate. What he had was a misunderstanding and a whole lot of money in REITs.

One of the most common questions (and it's one I wondered about, too, when I first started investing) is: **What's the difference between a REIT and a syndication?**

As it turns out, there aren't a *ton* of differences between a REIT and a syndication, but the differences that *do* exist are quite substantial.

That's not to say one is better than the other (though obviously we're biased toward syndications). Our goal in this section is to outline the major differences between these two investment vehicles so you can better understand how they fit into your portfolio.

What is a REIT?

REIT stands for Real Estate Investment Trust, and it's a company that owns and operates income-generating real estate. These companies tend to be quite large and they focus within a particular asset class (industrial, multifamily, retail, office).

Funding a REIT is modeled after mutual funds, where a group of investors pool capital. So far, this doesn't sound terribly different than a syndication, huh?

So let's get into the weeds and discuss the four differences between a REIT and an apartment syndication:

1. Ownership

The first thing to note is that, when you invest in a REIT, you're not actually investing in real estate, you're investing in a share of a company that owns and operates real estate. This is a subtle, but important, distinction (especially when it comes to the tax treatment of these vehicles).

Contrast this with investing in an apartment syndication whereby you and a group of investors each invest in an LLC, which in turn owns the real estate. As a result, direct ownership.

Here's another aspect to consider. When buying into REITs, you don't get a say in which properties are acquired. In fact, in many cases, it might be difficult to determine which buildings you've actually invested in. Your investment in these vehicles goes into what's known as a blind pool that the operators disburse at their discretion.

Some apartment syndications are structured in a similar way, but most are what we refer to as single asset acquisitions. When presented with one of these deals you are looking at only one property (or a portfolio of properties grouped together) and you get to underwrite and vet those properties on the individual level. If you don't like the location, business model, projected returns, or whatever, then you can opt out.

Not so with a REIT.

2. Liquidity

One of the strengths of a REIT is how easily you can buy and sell your shares.

Then again, one of the weaknesses of a REIT is also how easily you can buy and sell your shares.

Why is this both a strength and weakness?

Well it's obviously great for you if need quick access to your capital. If you need to free up some capital, no problem, just grab your phone and pop open your Vanguard app. You'll be liquid within a couple minutes.

Also, because REITs are publicly traded in the same way as stocks, it's incredibly easy to hop into this investment vehicle without having to plonk down tens of thousands of dollars.

So far these only sound like good things, right?

Not entirely. The sword cuts both ways, unfortunately. Because it's easy for *you* to buy and sell, it's also easy for everybody else to *buy* and *sell*. This means REITs are prone to the same volatility as the stock market, and a late-breaking news article or gang of Redditors can tank the value of your holding for no discernibly good underlying business reason.

Let's contrast that with apartment syndications.

First, syndications are notoriously difficult to get into. You either have to be an accredited investor (in which case you have access to a smorgasbord of potential private placements), or, if you're not part of the 10% of the population qualifying as an accredited investor, then you must establish a substantive preexisting relationship with an operator before you're allowed to hop into one of their deals.

Second, regardless of which class of investor you fall into, apartment syndications aren't something you can generally just jump into on a whim. Also, they're notoriously illiquid investments running on average between five and seven years. Oh yeah, and let's not forget that the minimum investment amount is usually around $50,000. That's a high hurdle for many people.

In exchange for the lack of convenience, apartment syndications are notoriously secure investments that do not see wild valuation swings overnight.

Which do you value more? Liquidity or stability?

How you answer that question will go a long way toward determining which of these investment vehicles is right for you.

3. Tax Benefits

It's not about what you make, it's about what you keep."

Your largest bill each year is likely to Uncle Sam. Nobody gets excited to pay taxes, but most people find the process to be so frustrating, obtuse, and demoralizing that they simply put it at the back of their mind until April 15th rolls around each year.

This head-in-the-sand method of wealth management won't do. Thankfully, there are some simple and easily accessible ways to reduce your taxable liabilities.

The most notable of these is by owning real estate.

There's a reason 80% of millionaires own investment real estate. Sure, the returns are great, but generally speaking, it's because the tax benefits are second to none.

Passive investors in an apartment syndication benefit from depreciation.

Depreciation, in the simplest terms, is the way the IRS recognizes that everything in this universe has a finite lifespan. This includes our buildings and everything comprising them.

Depreciation passes through to your K-1 (the tax return form you receive each year documenting how an investment performed) in the form of *losses*. These losses reduce your taxable liabilities on passively earned income, which, for our purposes here in an apartment syndication, would be the cash flow distributions.

So, if you invested in an apartment syndication, then at the end of the year it's likely you'll have earned some cash flow distributions. This very real income that hit your bank account will most likely be entirely offset by your share of the deprecation write-off.

The result? You pay nothing on the cash flow distributions until you sell the property and the depreciation is recaptured. In the meantime, that's tax-free income, baby.

Let's compare that to the tax treatment you'll receive investing in a REIT.

First, REITs do benefit from the power of depreciation, but this all occurs before the money ever hits your bank account. Sorry, you don't get the personal benefits of depreciation in a REIT.

Second, REITs pay out dividends, which are taxed as ordinary income. Depending on what tax bracket you're in, that can be a sizable chunk of change.

In short, not only do REITs *not* reduce your tax burden, they actually make it worse.

These taxes really take a bite out of what would otherwise be considered pretty good returns.

Speaking of returns... let's tackle that next because the amount you stand to make investing in a REIT versus an apartment syndication are pretty darn different.

4. Returns

Obviously returns vary by myriad factors, so let's take this section with a grain of salt. We're talking high-level averages here.

Historical data over the past twenty years shows REITs have outperformed the stock market, with an average annualized return of just under 12%.

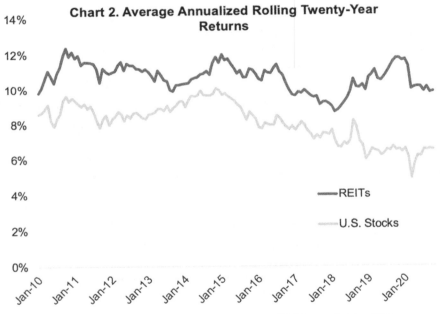

Chart 2. Average Annualized Rolling Twenty-Year Returns

Source: Nareit analysis of Factset monthly returns from January 1990 through October 2020.

That's not a terrible return, especially when compared against the stock market. It's important to note that these returns don't factor in tax treatment (as that's entirely variable depending on the individual). If taxes were factored into the returns, then the effective return of REITs would likely be around 8–9%.

Again, not terrible, but also not something you're likely to get too excited by, either.

Apartment syndications, by comparison, often generate well north of 20% average annual returns after cash flow, refinances, and sales are factored in. It's not uncommon to double your money in five years in an apartment syndication. A REIT, on the other hand, would likely take closer to eight years.

And once more, because it's so important and bears repeating, this doesn't take into consideration the tax benefits associated with owning *actual* real estate like you do in a syndication.

Okay, that horse is dead. We'll stop beating it now.

Should you invest in a REIT or an apartment syndication?

As with most things in life, there is no one-size-fits-all solution. Which investment vehicle is right for you ultimately depends on your unique goals and context.

If you're just starting your investing journey and only have a little capital to invest, a REIT might be your best option until you have saved enough to meet the $50,000 minimum investment most syndications require. A REIT might also be the right choice for you if you foresee needing your capital in the near future. Syndications are illiquid vehicles and your money will be tied up for between three and seven years in most cases. If you think you're going to need that money next year for your daughter's graduation, then a REIT, again, might be the right choice.

For us, syndications are our preferred choice of investment vehicle. I know, that's not terribly surprising. We're biased after all, but for good reason. Once you factor in the tax benefits, better returns, and additional security that comes from *knowing* the specific asset and the operating team, it's a no-brainer for us.

Let's finish this discussion of REITs versus apartment syndications by recalling the fact that life isn't binary and that there's nothing stopping you from diversifying into *both* investment vehicles. As the Buddhists would say, "The middle way *is* the way."

THE SIXTY-FIVE-POINT PASSIVE INVESTOR CHECKLIST

THE SPONSOR

Track Record: What is the sponsor's track record?

Personality: Do you know, like, and trust this sponsor?

Team: Who is on the sponsorship team? What skills and experience do they possess?

Strategy: What is their investing strategy/thesis?

References: Can the sponsor provide past investor or professional business references?

Skin in the Game: Is the sponsor contributing to the deal? If so, how much? If not, why not?

THE MARKET

Population Growth: Has this city shown consistent, strong growth (>20%) since 2000?

Job Growth: Has there been consistent job growth since 2000?

Economic Outlook: How strong/diverse is the current economic outlook? Is the market controlled predominately by one or two industries?

Unemployment Rate: What is the market's unemployment rate and how does that compare against national average and historical averages for that market?

Median Income: What is the median household income? What percentage of income is average rent? (<30% is desirable)

Crime Rate: What is the crime outlook for the submarket's neighborhood?

Rent Growth: What is the average rent growth for the past three years?

Occupancy Rates: What is the occupancy rate for the past three years? How does it compare to historical trends in that market?

Landlord vs. Tenant Friendly: Are the laws favorable to tenants or landlords?

THE PROPERTY

Year Built: What year was the property built?

Units: How many units does the property have?

Unit Mix: What is the mix of one-, two-, and three-bedroom units?

Price per Door: What is the price per door and how does that compare with the market average?

Building Class: What class is the building? (A, B, C, D)

Neighborhood Class: What class is the neighborhood? (A, B, C, D)

Current Occupancy: What is the current occupancy rate?

Concessions: How many concessions are being offered (e.g. free first month's rent)? Are these concessions comparable to nearby competitors?

Current vs. Market Rent: What is the current average rent and how does that compare to market average?

Amenities: What amenities does this property offer (pool, storage, dog park, laundry, etc.) and how does that compare to nearby competitors?

Mechanicals: How old are the mechanicals? (boiler, water heaters, A/C, electrical)

Roof: When was the roof replaced? What's its current condition?

Plumbing: What type of plumbing does the property have? Any known issues?

THE BUSINESS PLAN

The Plan: What is the business plan? (value-add, fix-and-flip, ground-up development, yield play)

Property Management: Who is the property management company? Do they have experience with this type of asset and business plan?

Capital Expenditures: How much is budgeted for CapEx? What improvements are planned?

Annual Rent Increase: What is the projected organic rent growth (1–3% is typically conservative)

Value-Add: How will value be added to this asset?

Vacancy Rates: What is the current physical and economic vacancy?

Cap Rate: What cap rate is the property being purchased at? What is current market cap rate for this asset class? What is the projected cap rate at disposition?

Rehab Budget / Unit: How much is budgeted for rehab per unit?

THE RETURNS

Projected Returns: What is the projected cash-on-cash return? What are the total projected returns? What is the projected internal rate of return? What is the projected equity multiple?

Equity Split: What is the equity split?

Distributions: How often will distributions be paid out? (monthly, quarterly, annually)

Preferred Return: Is there a preferred return? Does it roll over? Is it considered return *of* or *on* capital?

Minimum Investment: What is the minimum investment?

Hold Period: How long will the property be held?

506(b) vs. 506(c): Under which rule is this deal offered? Is it only open to accredited investors?

Retirement Funds: Can the investment be funded through a retirement plan? (self-directed IRA)

Distributions: How will investors receive distributions?

Fees: What is the acquisition fee? Asset management fee? Disposition fee? Construction management fee? Refinance fee? Loan guarantor fee? Disposition fee?

THE FINANCING

Loan Type: What is the loan type? (agency, bridge, portfolio)

Interest-Only Period: Is there an interest-only (IO) period?

Loan Term: What is the loan term?

Amortization Schedule: What is the amortization period?

Interest Rate: What is the interest rate? Is it fixed or adjustable?

Loan-to-Value: What is the loan-to-value (LTV)?

DSCR: What is the debt service coverage ratio?

Assumable: Is the loan assumable?

Recourse: Is the loan recourse or non-recourse?

Prepayment Penalty: Is there a prepayment penalty? If so, how is it calculated?

SAMPLE MARKETING PACKAGE

Familiarity breeds confidence, so we recommend taking a look at a few sample marketing packages before you evaluate your first actual deal.

Follow the link below to download a free copy of a sample marketing package.

www.invictusmultifamily.com/sample

An Investment Opportunity

Presented by

GLOSSARY OF TERMS

Absorption Rate – The rate at which available rentable units are leased in a specific market during a given time frame.

Accredited Investor – An individual that can invest in syndications by satisfying one of the requirements regarding income or net worth. The current requirements to qualify are an annual income of $200,000, or $300,000 for joint income, for the last two years with the expectation of earning the same or higher, or a net worth exceeding $1 million either individually or jointly with a spouse.

Acquisition Fee – Fee charged to cover commissions and expenses incurred in acquiring an asset. Typically between 1-3%.

Agency Loan – A long-term mortgage loan secured from Fannie Mae or Freddie Mac. Typical loan term lengths are 3, 5, 7, 10, 12 or more years amortized over up to 30 years. Apartment communities that are non-stabilized (85% occupancy or lower) will typically not qualify for agency debt.

Amortization – Spreading payments over multiple periods or allocating the cost of an intangible asset over a period of time.

Apartment Syndication – A partnership between active and passive investors to pool capital and intellectual resources to acquire, manage, and sell an apartment community while sharing in the profits.

Appraisal – A report created by a certified appraiser that specifies the market value of a property. Apartment values are calculated by cost, income, and sales comparison approaches.

Asset Management Fee – Fee charged to manage an asset over the life of a hold. Typically between 1-2%.

Average Annual Return (AAR) – A percentage used when reporting the historical return of an investment. Calculated by dividing the total yearly returns by the number of years invested.

Bad Debt – The amount of uncollected money owed by a tenant after move-out.

Break Even Occupancy – The minimum occupancy rate required to cover all property expenses.

Bridge Loan – A mortgage loan used until a borrower secures permanent financing. Bridge loans have shorter terms, higher interest rates, and usually include favorable interest-only periods. These loans are ideal for repositioning an apartment building that doesn't qualify for permanent financing.

Capitalization Rate (Cap Rate) – The expected market return of an investment property purchased entirely in cash. Calculated by dividing the Net Operating Income of an asset by it's Current Market Value or Sales Price.

Capital Expenditures (CapEx) – The funds used to acquire, upgrade, and maintain a property. An expense is considered CapEx when it improves the useful life of a property.

Cashflow – The revenue remaining after paying all expenses. Calculated by subtracting the operating expenses and debt service from effective gross income.

Cash on Cash Return (COC) – The rate of return achieved in relation to the initial cash invested. Calculated by dividing cash invested by cashflow before tax.

Closing Costs – The expenses over and above the price of the property that buyers and sellers pay to complete a real estate transaction. Costs incurred may include loan origination fees, discount points, appraisal fees, title searches, title insurance, surveys, taxes, deed-recording fees and credit report charges.

Concessions – The credits given to offset rent, application fees, move-in fees, and any other cost incurred by the tenant, which are given at move-in to entice tenants into signing a lease.

Cost Segregation Study – Identifies and reclassifies personal property assets to shorten the depreciation time for taxation purposes, which reduces current income tax obligations.

Cost Approach – A method of calculating a property's value based on the cost to replace (or rebuild) the property from scratch. Also referred to as replacement cost.

Debt Service – The amount of money required over a period of time to repay debts.

Debt Service Coverage Ratio (DSCR) – A measure of the cashflow available to pay current debt obligations. Formula: Net Operating Income (NOI) divided by Total Debt Service

Depreciation – A reduction in the value of an asset with the passage of time, due in particular to wear and tear.

Disposition Fee – A fee charged for services rendered in an investment disposition, including sales marketing, negotiating and closing of the deal.

Distressed Property – A non-stabilized apartment building, which means economic occupancy rate is below 85%.

Distributions – The limited partners' portion of the profits, which are sent on a monthly, quarterly, or annual basis, at refinance, and/or at sale.

Due Diligence – The process of confirming a property is as represented by the seller and is not subject to environmental or other problems.

Earnest Money Deposit (EMD) – Deposit made to the seller indicating buyer's good faith, ranges anywhere from 1-5% purchase price.

Economic Occupancy – Refers to the proportion of the Gross Potential Income (GPI) that is collected, the money that is actually paid. Formula: Total rents collected divided by total rents scheduled

Effective Gross Income (EGI) – The Gross Potential Income less vacancy and collection losses.

Equity Investment – The upfront costs for purchasing a property. These costs include the down payment for the mortgage loan, closing costs, financing fees, operating account funding, capital expenditures (if excluded from the loan) and the fees paid to the general partnership for putting the deal together.

Equity Multiple (EM) – The rate of return based on the total net profit and the equity investment. Formula: Divide the sum of the total net profit (cashflow + sales proceeds) and the remaining equity investment at sale by the equity investment

Environmental Site Assessment (ESA) – A report prepared for a real estate holding that identifies potential or existing environmental contamination liabilities. The Phase I ESA is the first step in the process of environmental due diligence.

Financing Fees – The one-time, upfront fees charged by the lender for providing the debt service.

General Partner (GP) – An owner of a partnership who has unlimited liability. A GP is a managing partner and is active in the day-to-day operations of the business. In apartment syndications, the GP is also referred to as the sponsor, operator, or syndicator.

Gross Potential Income (GPI) – The total rent a property can generate if 100% leased at market rent.

Gross Rent Multiplier (GRM) – The ratio of the price of a real estate investment to its annual rental income before accounting for expenses, it is the number of years the property would take to pay for itself in gross received rents. Formula: Selling price or value divided by gross rents.

Guaranty Fee – A fee paid to a loan guarantor at closing for signing for and guaranteeing the loan.

Holding Period – The amount of time the asset will be owned.

Income Approach – A method of calculating an apartment's value based on the capitalization rate and the net operating income (value = net operating income/capitalization rate).

Interest Only (I/O) – A period of time in which the borrower only pays the interest on the mortgage through monthly payments.

Interest Rate – The amount charged by a lender to a borrower for the use of their funds.

Internal Rate of Return (IRR) – The rate needed to convert the sum of all future uneven cashflow to equal the initial equity investment. That "uneven cashflow" can be cashflow, sales proceeds and principal pay down.

Investing (Active) – The finding of, qualifying, and closing on a real estate asset using one's own capital and overseeing the business plan through to its successful execution.

Investing (Passive) – Placing one's capital into an apartment syndication or other real estate investment that is managed in its entirety by a general partner.

Lease – A formal legal contract between a landlord and a tenant for occupying an apartment unit for a specified time and at a specified rent with specified terms.

Loan to Value (LTV) – The ratio of a loan to the value of an asset purchased. Formula: Mortgage lien divided by the appraised value of the property

Loan to Cost (LTC) – The ratio of a loan to the cost of building the project. Formula: Mortgage lien divided by the appraised value of the property plus the cost of building the project.

Letter of Intent (LOI) – A non-binding agreement stating two or more parties' desire to enter into a real estate transaction.

Limited Partner (LP) – A partner whose liability is limited to the extent of their share of ownership. In apartment syndications, the LP is the passive investor who funds a portion of the equity investment.

Loss-to-Lease (LtL) – The revenue lost based on the market rent and the actual rent. Formula: Divide the gross potential rent minus the actual rent collect by the gross potential rent

Market Rent – The rent amount a willing landlord might reasonably expect to receive and a willing tenant might reasonably expect to pay for tenancy, which is based on the rent charged at similar apartment communities in the area. The market rent is typically calculated by conducting a rent comparable analysis.

Metropolitan Statistical Area (MSA) – A geographical region containing a substantial population nucleus, together with adjacent communities having a high degree of economic and social integration with that core. MSA's are determined by the United States Office of Management and Budget (OMB).

Mortgage – A legal contract by which an apartment is pledged as security for repayment of a loan until the debt is repaid in full.

Net Operating Income (NOI) – Equals all revenue from the property minus all operating expenses. NOI is a before-tax figure which excludes principal and interest payments on loans, capital expenditures, depreciation and amortization. Formula: Net Income minus Operating Expenses

Non-recourse Loan – The right of the lender to go after personal assets above and beyond the collateral if the borrower defaults on the loan AND a carve-out is triggered (i.e. gross negligence or fraud).

Occupancy (Economic) – The rate of paying tenants based on the total possible revenue and the actual revenue collected. Formula: Divide the effective gross income by the gross potential income

Occupancy (Physical) – The proportion of occupied units. Formula: Divide the total number of occupied units by the total number of units at the property

Operating Agreement – A document that outlines the responsibilities and ownership percentages for the general and limited partners in an apartment syndication.

Operating Expenses – The costs of running and maintaining the property. For apartment syndications, the operating expenses are usually broken into the following categories; payroll, maintenance and repairs, contract services, make ready, advertising/marketing, administrative, utilities, management fees, taxes, insurance, and reserves.

Physical Occupancy – The rate of occupied units. The physical occupancy rate is calculated by dividing the total number of occupied units by the total number of units at the property.

Preferred Return – Refers to the ordering in which profits are distributed to investors. Preferred returns means contractual entitlement to distributions of profit until a threshold rate of return has been met, before profit distributions are made to any other subordinate stakeholders.

Prepayment Penalty – A clause in a mortgage contract stating that a penalty will be assessed if the mortgage is paid down or paid off within a certain period.

Price Per Unit – The cost per unit of purchasing a property. The price per unit is calculated by dividing the purchase price of the property by the total number of units.

Principal – The original sum lent to the borrower.

Private Placement Memorandum (PPM) – A legal document provided to prospective investors when selling securities that states the objectives, risks and terms of an investment.

Pro Forma – The projected budget with itemized line items for the revenue and expenses for the next 12-months and/or the next 5 years.

Profit and Loss Statement (T-12) – A document or spreadsheet containing detailed information about the revenue and expenses of an apartment over the last 12 months. Also referred to as a trailing 12-month profit and loss statement, P&L, operating statement, or T-12.

Purchase & Sale Agreement (PSA) – The agreement that finalizes all terms and conditions in the buying/selling of an asset as originally stipulated in the Letter of Intent (LOI).

Property and Neighborhood Classes – A ranking system of A, B, C, or D assigned to a property and a neighborhood based on a variety of factors. For property classes, these factors include date of construction, condition of the property and amenities offered. For neighborhood classes, these factors include demographics, median income and median home values, crime rates and school district rankings.

Property Management Fee – An ongoing monthly fee paid to the property management company for managing the day-to-day operations of the property including leasing, repairs, and rent collection.

Ratio Utility Billing System (RUBS) – A method of calculating a resident's utility bill based on occupancy, apartment square footage, number of beds, or some combination of factors less a predetermined percentage of a common area allowance.

Recourse Loan – The right of the lender to go after personal assets above and beyond the collateral if the borrower defaults on the loan.

Refinance Fee – A fee charged for services rendered the case of a refinance of the deal.

Rent Comparable Analysis (Rent Comps) – The process of analyzing the rental rates of similar properties in the area to determine the market rents of the units at the subject property.

Rent Premium – The increase in rent demanded after performing renovations to the interior and/or exterior of an apartment community.

Rent Roll – A document or spreadsheet containing detailed information on each of the units at the apartment community, including the unit number, unit type, square footage, tenant name, market rent, actual rent, security deposit amount, move-in date, lease-start and lease-end dates, and the tenant's balance.

Sales Comparison Approach – A method of calculating an apartment's value based on similar apartments recently sold in a particular region.

Sophisticated Investor – A person who is deemed to have sufficient investing experience and knowledge to weigh the risks and merits of an investment opportunity but does not meet the accredited investor qualifications.

Subscription Agreement – A document that is a promise by the LLC that owns the property to sell a specific number of shares to a limited partner at a specified price, and a promise by the limited partner to pay that price.

Submarket – A geographic subdivision of a market.

Syndication – The transfer of something for control or management by a group of individuals or organizations.

Underwriting – The process in which an underwriter researches and assesses the risk of a potential asset.

Vacancy Loss – The amount of revenue lost due to unoccupied units.

Vacancy Rate – The proportion of unoccupied units. Formula: Divide the total number of unoccupied units by the total number of units.

Loan (Permanent Agency) – A long-term mortgage loan secured from Fannie Mae or Freddie Mac. Typical loan term lengths are 3, 5, 7, 10, 12 or more years amortized over up to 30 years. Apartment communities that are non-stabilized (85% occupancy or lower) will typically not qualify for agency debt.

Value-Add Property – A stabilized apartment community with an economic occupancy above 85% and has an opportunity to be improved by adding value, which means making improvements to the operations and the physical property through exterior and interior renovations in order to increase the income and/or decrease the expenses.

Waterfall – A method by which the capital gained by the fund is allocated between the limited partners (LPs) and the general partner (GP).

Yield Maintenance – A penalty paid by the borrower on a loan if the principal is paid off early.

ABOUT INVICTUS CAPITAL

Invictus Capital specializes in acquiring and operating value-add multi-family properties in Minneapolis and Saint Paul, MN that deliver cashflow from day one, the opportunity for significant forced-appreciation, and excellent tax benefits to our passive investors.

THE PARTNERS

Anthony Vicino is a serial entrepreneur who has helped build multiple multi-million dollar companies from the ground-up by creating efficient systems that scale, by utilizing value-based content marketing strategies, and by focusing on providing exceptional end-user experiences.

He is a Best-Selling Author, Investor, and Small Business Owner who successfully managed his own personal portfolio of multifamily assets spread across the country before joining forces with Dan Krueger in 2019 to create Invictus Capital.

Together, Anthony and Dan, are driven to help people achieve financial security by providing solid multifamily-based investment opportunities in an environment of trust, transparency, and clarity.

Dan Krueger is a full-time entrepreneur, investor, and coach who is passionate about helping others become financially free by investing in apartment buildings.

Besides providing lucrative investment opportunities, his mission is to help educate investors in financial literacy so they can take control of their financial future.

Before beginning his full-time career in real estate investing, Dan spent 5 years in corporate finance where he managed the operating expenses for multinational fortune 500 companies.

Since then, he has grown his real estate portfolio by more than 500% annually.

LEARN MORE FROM JAKE & GINO

And become Successful in Your Real Estate Business Today

If you've enjoyed this book, we hope you will take a moment to check out some of our additional resources that we offer at *www.jakeandgino.com*.

Jake & Gino is a multifamily community created to teach investors how to become multifamily entrepreneurs by engaging with other members and accessing their weekly podcasts, blogs, and training videos.

To begin your journey with Jake & Gino, visit *Become A Member*

MORE FROM JAKE & GINO PUBLISHING

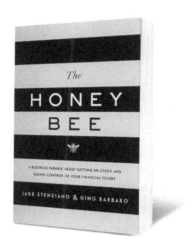

THE HONEY BEE

A business parable that teaches the value of cultivating multiple streams of income, the Honey Bee tells the story of Noah, a disappointed, disaffected salesman who feels like his life is going nowhere until the day he has a chance encounter with a man named Tom Barnham, the beekeeper. In his charming, down-home way, Tom the "Bee-Man" teaches Noah and his wife Emma how to grow their personal wealth using the lessons he learned from his beekeeping passion.

For more information, visit *www.jakeandgino.com/honeybee*

CREATIVE CASH

Creative Cash was written to eliminate this limiting belief by diving into two very effective creative financing strategies that most new investors are unaware of: Master Lease Options and Seller Financing. These two strategies allowed the author Bill Ham to purchase his first four hundred units without stepping into a bank and qualifying for a loan.

Bill lays out his step-by-step framework to:

- How to buy a property without having to step inside a bank.

- How to find a deal.

- How to analyze and underwrite a deal.

- How to select an emerging market.

- How to make offers and perform due diligence.

For more information, visit *www.creativeapartmentdeals.com*

PASSIVE INVESTING MADE SIMPLE

Want to take your education into passive investing even deeper?

Take the Passive Investing Made Simple Master Class, available at:

www.thepassiveinvestingbook.com

Jam-packed with over ten hours' worth of video content, a workbook, and direct 1-on-1 access with the authors, Anthony Vicino and Dan Krueger, this master class is designed to take your passive investing game to the next level.

Sign up today!

Made in the USA
Las Vegas, NV
14 August 2021

28184431R00174